Otto Locke

Comal Springs Nursery materials

Otto Locke

Comal Springs Nursery materials

ISBN/EAN: 9783741136207

Manufactured in Europe, USA, Canada, Australia, Japa

Cover: Foto ©Thomas Meinert / pixelio.de

Manufactured and distributed by brebook publishing software
(www.brebook.com)

Otto Locke

Comal Springs Nursery materials

1903—SEASON—1904

COMAL SPRINGS NURSERY

OTTO LOCKE, Proprietor,

New Braunfels,   -   -   Texas

Johnson Bros Ptg. Co., San Antonio, Texas

Greeting:

Another season has come to an end. It has been a very prosperous one, and I am sending to you herewith my eighteenth annual catalogue, thanking you through these lines for the liberal way in which you have patronized me, and for the kind words which all of my customers put in for me whenever and wherever an occasion presents itself.

This booklet has for many years been a true and faithful guide to many tree planters and I hope it may do as much good in the future as it has done in the past, in helping the planter in his selection of proper varieties.

It does not contain as many novelties in the fruit line as usual, for the reason that there are very few new fruits worthy of introduction, but of roses and ornamentals you will find a good many not heretofore described in this book.

The growing season has been an exceptionally favorable one for nursery stock, and everything is of good size, in healthy condition, and exceedingly fine looking.

EMIL LOCKE   OTTO LOCKE   HERMAN LOCKE

THESE THREE MEN GROW YOUR TREES

Fruit Trees.

.. .. ..

Apples.

Prices: Strong, 4 to 6 feet, grafted on whole roots, 15 cents; $10 per 100.
Extra large selected trees and new varieties 25 cents each.

The apple is not very profitably grown in Southern and Western Texas. There are few varieties that grow, and only certain localities where these succeed. The latter are in the mountainous regions of Texas and Mexico. The best results are obtained on heavy clay soil. Light or sandy soil must be manured before apples can successfully be grown on same. The apple we grow in our state has a very fine aromatic flavor, more so than that grown in the North, and people who think that their soil may be adapted to its culture should experiment with a few trees. Trees grown in the North should, however, never be planted; they will never prove a success.

The following is a collection of those that I have found worthy of planting in the South:

Der Apfel ist nicht sehr profitabel in Süd= und West = Texas und sind es nur wenige Sorten, die gedeihen. Auf den Gebirgshöhen und Lande mit reichem Lehmboden bringt der Apfelbaum die reichsten Ernten. Ist der Boden leicht und sandig, so sollte tüchtig gedüngt werden. Der Apfel, der in unserem Klima gezogen wird, hat ein sehr reiches Aroma und ist als Tafel = Obst beliebt. Bäume, die aus dem Norden stammen, sollten niemals gepflanzt werden, da sie nie gedeihen.

Folgende sind die besten Sorten für den Süden :

Red June, medium to large, oblong, dark red, crisp, sometimes almost mealy tender, high flavored. Ripe June 5, and sometimes until July.

Red Astrachan, large size, crimson and yellow, juicy, crisp, valuable for cooking; tree a fine grower and very prolific. June 1 to July 15.

Yellow Transparent, Russian variety, medium, pale yellow; early.

Yellow Horse, known throughout the South as the best all-purpose summer apple, large, yellow, sometimes with red blush, firm, splendid for cooking, eating and drying. August 15.

Fall Queen, tree upright, spreading and long-lived, fruit large, yellow with bright red cheeks, very rich and juicy. September and October.

Kinnard's Choice, fruit medium, mostly covered with a dark red, flesh yellow, tender, juicy and aromatic; very hardy and productive.

Winesap, tree a strong grower and productive, fruit of medium size, red flesh, crisp, juicy, high flavored, valuable for table, market and cider. Ripe in October.

Black Twig, tree upright grower, fruit like Winesap, but one-fourth larger.

Ben Davis, everyone has seen this apple, as it is sold by grocers in fall and winter; large, red and yellow striped, subacid, valuable. October.

Hershal Cox, a new winter apple from Tennessee; fruit and tree resemble Ben Davis, but fruit smaller, better quality and better keeper.

Bismarck, this most valuable New Zealand apple was introduced only a few years ago, and the popularity it is now enjoying is proof enough of its great value. It not only possesses high quality, but the tree is very hardy; just the apple for our climate. 25 cents each.

McKinley Greening, an apple which I have not tried myself, but which comes to me described as follows: Tree slow grower, but fruit the very finest yellow imaginable, and keeps all winter. I shall give it a fair trial here, and have some trees for my customers out West, who have better soil for apples. 20 cents each.

Heidemeyer, imported about 1850 from Stuttgart, Germany. Roundish, conical, color golden yellow, flesh yellowish, juicy, aromatic, rich quality, very good to best. Season August, bears heavy crops every year; it is one of the best apples for Southwest Texas. Price 25 cents.

Crab Apples.

Price, two-year-old trees, 15 cents each.

This pretty little apple is especially adapted for preserves and is always sure to bring a good crop.

Dieſer ſchöne, kleine Apfel iſt als Preſerve ſehr beliebt und bringt immer ſichere, reiche Ernten. Der Baum wächſt ſchnell und kräftig.

Hyslop, ornamental as well as useful. Vigorously growing tree, produces in great abundance crimson apples. Fruit good for preserves.

Transcendant (Siberian), an attractive yellow color, splashed and striped with red; bears very young, annual crops thereafter. We value it highly for preserves. Buds and blossoms exquisitely beautiful. Ripens in July.

Whitney No. 20, this is the best of all the crab apples as far as the quality of the fruit is concerned, fruit is of good size, very sweet and aromatic. Tree upright grower and very regular bearer, and succeeds remarkably well with me. Color of fruit yellow with heavy crimson stripes. 20 cents each.

Yates, bright red covered with white specks; quality fine, very productive, long keeper. This is one of the best apples known.

A FOUR-YEAR-OLD SUMMER BEAUTY PEAR TREE IN BEARING;

Pears.

In order of ripening. Two-year-old trees, 25 cents each; $2.50 per 12, $20 per 100. Extra large and new varieties, 6 to 7 feet, 50 cents.

The pear is the most profitable fruit we know of. After a tree has once begun to bear, it will bear regularly every year. The tree is very long-lived if it has a favorable locality where it can send its roots deep into the ground for a supply of moisture; for this reason pear trees should only be planted where the subsoil is rich and deep.

The soil most adapted to pear culture is rich loam, which contains a good supply of humus. Sandy soil with clay subsoil is also good if well manured. Pear trees should however never be planted on soil where roots of cotton and potatoes rot, as such soil has the same effect upon pear trees.

The following are the best varieties:

Die Birne ist die profitabelste von allen hier bekannten Obstarten, da sie immer sichere Ernten bringt. Die Wurzel des Birn-Baumes geht tief in das Erdreich hinein und dort, wo guter, tiefer Untergrund ist und die Wurzel ge= nügend Feuchtigkeit findet, erreicht der Baum ein hohes Alter und bringt sichere, reiche Ernten. Eine gute, reife Birne wird fast von einem Jeden anderem Obst vorgezogen. Man pflanze aber ja keinen Birn = Baum auf Boden, wo Wurzelsäule (root rot) ist, dort stirbt der Birn = Baum ab. Die Birne ge= deiht am besten auf humusreichem, schwarzem oder Lehmboden ; doch auch auf Sandboden mit Lehm=Untergrund wird sie mit dem allerbesten Erfolg gezogen. Folgende sind die besten Sorten :

Koonce, (new), very early, of the very best quality, does not rot at the core. The fruit is of a straw color with red cheeks and brown dots. Tree of vigorous growth, healthy, and very hardy in bud and bloom, so that late frosts will not kill the blossoms.

Early Harvest, fruit medium to large, skin pale yellow, with blush next to sun, flesh white, tender, sweet; one of the best of its season. July.

Clapp's Favorite, prolific, red cheek, large, excellent, one of the best table pears.

Summer Beauty, first raised in 1873, and introduced in 1893 by us. This pear is the finest fruit and the surest bearer of all varieties that ever have been tested so far south. The trees have not failed to produce heavy crops every year since 1880. It is a vigorous, symmetrical grower and late bloomer, so that spring frosts will not injure it. The fruit is very large and handsome, of yellow color with a bright red cheek, flavor sweet, sugary, rich, aromatic, and pleasant, excellent quality, always grows in clusters of from three to five. One of the rarest and most productive pears in cultiva- tion. Ripening the end of July. Price of well rooted one-year-old trees, 50 cents each.

Flemish Beauty, medium, beautiful, juicy, melting, rich and firm, does well here.

Bartlett, Every one is acquainted with this large yellow pear. Fruit is very rich and highly aromatic, the reason why this pear can always be sold while others may be refused. Tree grows dense, and of even and conical shape.

Buffum, medium size, yellow shaded with reddish brown and russet; sweet and fine. Ripens in August and September.

Howell, large waxen yellow with red cheeks, rich, buttery, sweet and perfumed, strong grower, productive and valuable.

Smith's Hybrid, is one of our best pears. We consider it better than LeConte in quality, and being earlier it brings a better price in market. The fruit is larger than LeConte.

LeConte, of remarkable vigor and beauty of growth. The fruit is bell-shaped; of a rich creamy yellow when ripe; very smooth and fine looking, and a good shipper.

Duchess, pale yellow, very large; has a peculiar taste for which many people prefer it to other pears.

Winter Butter, This new and very valuable pear was imported by us from Falkenau, Sachsen (Germany), several years ago. It is the finest pear found on the markets of Falkenau, and commands the very highest price there. My young trees in the orchard are doing fine, and I feel quite sure that this will add a very valuable variety to our list of pears for the market. I have very fine young trees for sale, and every lover of fine fruit should experiment with a few trees. 50 cts. each.

Kieffer Hybrid, called by many the "Queen of Pears." Fruit large to very large, skin yellow, with a brilliant vermillion cheek, flesh brittle, very juicy, with a marked musky aroma. Tree very vigorous and very prolific. Considered the best all-around pear.

Magnolia, a distinct variety of the oriental type, introduced by the Alabama and Georgia Nurseries. The bark of the tree is very dark, covered with white specks. Fruit also very large, brown and red color. Ripens Ripens shortly after Kieffer. 50 cents each.

Garber Hybrid, oriental strain, like the Smith's, fruit resembles the Kieffer in size, shape and color, ripe three weeks later.

Quinces.

25 cents each; $2.50 per 12.

The quince likes a rich, deep, moist and at the same time loose soil and requires careful cultivation. The fruit is only used in a cooked state and it is a great favorite with the housewife, owing to its rich aroma, which makes it fit for all kinds of preserves and jellies.

Die Quitte liebt einen sehr reichen, tiefen, losen Boden und gebraucht eine sorgfältige Kultur. Die Frucht wird nur gekocht genossen, da sie roh hart und holzig ist. Sie ist bei der Hausfrau sehr beliebt, da sie ein feines Aroma hat und wird beim Einkochen von anderem Obst verwendet, da sie demselben einen feinen Geschmack giebt.

Orange, large, roundish, bright golden yellow, cooks tender, and is of excellent flavor. Valuable for preserves and flavoring, very productive; one of the most popular and extensively cultivated of old varieties. Ripens in October.

Champion, fruit very large, fair and handsome. Tree very productive, bears when young, flesh cooks as tender as the apple, flavor very delicate, imparting an exquisite taste and odor to any fruit with which it is cooked.

Meech's, a vigorous grower and immensely productive. The fruit is large, orange yellow, of great beauty and delightful fragrance. Excellent for cooking.

Almonds.

Two-year-old trees, 25 cents each; one-year-old trees, 20 cents each.

The almond succeeds in Western Texas, Arizona, New and Old Mexico and California, where irrigation is practicable. As the tree blooms very early the crops are often destroyed by late frosts.

Die Mandel gedeiht mit Bewässerung in West-Teras, Meriko, Arizona und Californien. Da sie sehr früh blüht, so wird die Ernte häufig durch Spät= Fröste zerstört.

Sultana, large kernels, soft shells. Tree is a strong, upright grower.

I have a few other varieties, as **Princess, Languadoc and Nonpareil.**

Apricots.

In order of ripening. 25 cents each, $2.50 per 12.

Two-year-old trees, extra large, 35 cents each, $3.50 per 12.

The apricot is one of those fruits that do fairly well on limestone soil; a rich, heavy soil, however, is preferred. As the apricot blooms early, it should not be planted extensively in localities visited by late frosts. The fruit is much beloved for its rich and aromatic flavor, and the apricot should be represented by a few trees, at least, in every garden.

The culture is about the same as that of the peach.

Die Aprikose gedeiht gut auf Kalkboden auch liebt sie einen mehr festen als losen Boden. Sie blüht früh und ist die Ernte nicht immer sicher, da sie oft durch Spätfrost zerstört wird. Es ist die erste Frucht die reift und von einem köstlichen Aroma. Ein Jeder sollte einige Bäume dieser lieblichen Frucht an= pflanzen. Der Baum sollte wie ein Pfirsich=Baum behandelt werden.

Royal, fruit large, oval; color of skin dull yellow, tinted with red on the sunny side; flesh pale orange color, firm, juicy, rich and vinous freestone. Ripens end of June.

Meyer's Early, ripens early in May, is of medium size and of white color.

Eureka, very early, large, fine, prolific.

Blendheim, Russian, large, golden yellow with a red check, good qual- ity, bears well.

Moorpark, large, excellent, an old favorite and one of the best bearers. This is the best of all apricots.

Cluster, of beautiful, symmetrical growth, very vigorous and hardy, fruit medium, transparent yellow.

Cherries.

35 cents each.

The cherry succeeds well on the elevated plateaus of Texas, New Mex- ico, Arizona, California and Mexico. We should, however, not recommend its planting in the lowlands.

The following varieties have proved the most successful in the South:

Die Kirsche gedeiht auf reichem Boden der Höhenzüge von Texas, Merito und Californien; trägt aber sehr selten in den Niederungen von Süd= und West=Texas. Folgende Sorten sind die profitabelsten:

Early Richmond, medium, red, juicy, rich, acid, one of the most valuable cherries for this climate.

Large Montmorency, fruit very large, color red, flavor acid.

Ostheimer (Russian), slender grower, very hardy; of good size and quality, productive. June.

Black Tartarian, very large, purplish black, half tender, flavor mild and pleasant. Tree remarkably vigorous, erect, beautiful grower and very popular. May and June.

Nectarines.

25 cents each.

The nectarine is a fruit similar to a peach, but it has a smooth skin like that of a plum. It is successfully grown in some parts of Texas, Mexico and California.

Die Nectarine ist eine Frucht der Pfirsich ähnlich, doch mit glatter Schale wie die Pflaume. Gedeiht gut in Texas, Theilen von Merito und Californien.

Honey, originated in our nursery and named after its parent, the Honey peach. It is the only prolific nectarine we have so far grown here, and fruit is of very good quality; it is larger than the Honey peach, just as sweet, and ripens beginning of July; color of fruit is yellow with blush cheeks, flesh very tender and white. We have a few June budded trees of this variety at 50 cents each.

Boston, large, deep yellow, with a bright blush and mottling of red, sweet and a peculiar pleasant flavor. Freestone.

Coosa, very large, red, flesh white; a new seedling from upper Georgia.

Victoria, medium, purple, brown cheek.

Jumbo, originated in Burnett county from a peach seed. Fruit is very large and of a rich yellow color.

Figs.

20 cents each, $15 per hundred.

We might almost say there is no tree which so abundantly repays its owner for the little trouble it requires than the fig. From July to October ripe fruit may be had almost daily from the same tree, provided there is enough moisture to constantly keep the tree growing during this time.

The best place for a fig tree is near a well or a spring or any other place where there is always a plentiful supply of water. During extreme cold weather figs sometimes freeze to the ground, but they sprout from the roots again in the spring. This, however, happens only every 10 or 15 years, if only the hardiest varieties are planted.

Wohl keine Obstart bringt hier im Süden so reiche Ernten als die Feige. Von Juli bis Ende Oktober kann man täglich reife Früchte von einem Feigen= Baum pflücken, wenn er genügend Feuchtigkeit hat um um beständig wachsen zu können. Die Feige sollte an Brunnen, Quellen oder dort, wo der Boden be= ständig feucht ist, angepflanzt werden. Es kommt vor, daß die Feigen=Bäume in strengen Wintern bis auf den Boden abfrieren, sie treiben aber im Früh= jahr immer wieder von neuem aus den Wurzeln.

Green Ischia, green, medium size, of excellent quality.

Magnolia, large, rich fruit, yellowish white. Hardy here. Small one year plants bear fruit first summer.

Brown Turkey, medium, brown, very sweet and excellent; very prolific and hardy. The most reliable fig for open field culture.

Brunswick, brown or violet, quality excellent.

Celestial, small, pale violet, with bloom; very sweet, prolific and hardy.

Peaches.

In order of ripening. 4 to 6 feet, 15 cents each; $10 per 100, except where noted. Extra large, selected trees, 25 cents each. 2 and 3 years, bearing age, well headed trees, 50 cts. each, $5 per dozen.

The peach is probably more extensively cultivated in our country than any other fruit, and it well deserves its popularity amongst the American people, as there is nothing that excels a luscious, red-ripe peach. There has however been much complaint of late that the finer varieties do not bear enough in Texas. People attribute this to the drought, yet the failure in most cases is due to the ignorance of the people. The traveling tree agents from other states introduce new varieties every year that are in most cases not at all adapted to our climate. Therefore, never buy a tree unless you know that it is grown by a reliable nurseryman in your own state. West Texas is a dry country, but nevertheless good peaches can be raised, and plenty of them, provided the proper varieties are planted.

The peach succeeds in almost any soil, but it prefers sandy soil with red clay subsoil to any other.

The following varieties are all thoroughly tested by me, and I

OUR TWO-YEAR-OLD PEACH TREES

consider them the best collection that can be made for our climate. They are selected from 400 different varieties, and as each variety has a ripening period of from 10 to 15 days, peaches may be had all the time from the middle of May until November. I have arranged them in order of ripening for the convenience of the buyer.

Die Pfirſich iſt die am meiſten hier angepflanzte Obſtart und das mit Recht, denn nichts geht über eine gute, reife, ſaftige Pfirſich. Leider wird die letzten Jahre ſo viel geklagt, daß die Bäume keine Früchte tragen, zum Theil wird wohl die Trockenheit Schuld haben, aber die größte Schuld liegt daran, daß durch die Baum-Agenten Bäume maſſenhaft in den Markt gebracht werden, die im Norden oder Californien gezogen wurden ; ſolche Bäume wachſen ſehr gut aber bringen höchſt ſelten Frucht, desbalb pflanzt niemals Pfirſich = Bäume, wenn ihr nicht beſtimmt wißt, daß ſie im Süden gezogen ſind. Die hier fol= genden Sorten ſind die beſten aus nahezu 400 Sorten, welche ich die letzten 15 Jahre hindurch verſucht habe. Jede Sorte hat eine Reifezeit von 10 bis 15 Tagen und in dieſer Liſte ſind alle Sorten enthalten, die von Mitte Mai bis November reifen. Der Pfirſich-Baum gedeiht auf faſt jedem Boden, am beſten auf Sandboden mit rothem Lehm als Untergrund.

I. Ripening here from May 20 to June 10.

Victor. My young trees bore their second crop this season and I am highly pleased with the fruit, which is round in shape, and of beautiful color. Flesh is white, crisp and very juicy.

Sneed, ripe 10 days before Alexander, of Chinese type. Tree of vigorous growth and drooping habit.

Greensboro (new), earlier and larger than Alexander, fine flavor and attractive appearance.

Dwarf Japan Blood, Tree of dwarf habit, surest bearer of all the early peaches. Fruit is large, pointed, red cheek and end, and sometimes blood-red flesh.

Alexander, good quality, high color, flesh greenish white. Best bearing May peach.

Jessie Kerr, originated from seed of Hale's Early; about the size of and season with Alexander, bears well.

Triumph "The earliest yellow peach in the world." A perfect yellow free-stone, of excellent quality. Ripens after Alexander. A good keeper, very prolific. Two-year-old trees bore ½ bushel each.

Carman, (new), the best Texas Seedling Peach, size very large and of finest flavor, ripening after Alexander, vigorous, prolific.

Bokara, the hardiest peach known. It is of fine quality and a good bearer. Does remarkably well here.

Honey, the sweetest of all peaches we have and about the best bearer. Late frosts have never killed the young fruit here. Color is attractive and it always sells easily. Honey is about the best peach for general planting we have.

II. Ripening June 5 to 20.

Early Rivers, large, light straw color, with a pink cheek; fleshy, juicy and melting, with a rich flavor. One of the beautiful early peaches. Free-stone.

Southern Early, this is the largest of all early peaches, good quality, very prolific, sweet and juicy.

Pearson, similar to Mamie Rose, but as large as Chinese Cling. A perfect freestone, ripe before Mamie Rose. It is a hardy, prolific and a very valuable new peach.

June Rose, a large peach with a red cheek and white flesh. Very juicy and well flavored. Tree latest bloomer.

Rogers, extra large, red cheek, juicy, aromatic, sure bearer. A seedling of Chinese Cling and one of our best peaches.

Yellow Mystery, yellow freestone, early, a good bearer.

George the 4th, large, flesh white, red cheek, productive, a good freestone.

Husted Early, large size. In shape roundish, skin smooth and of light yellow color, with a beautiful red cheek on the sunny side. Flesh light cream color, flavor rich and delicious, melting, juicy and vinous.

Bishop, a very large crimson peach with white flesh. It is a good bearer.

Aurora, very large, globular, red cheek to the sunny side, juicy and of good flavor, bears well. A fine new peach, freestone.

Cleveland Free, a seedling of Thurber. Fruit large, creamy white, red cheek, juicy, rich and excellent.

Lady Ingold, very large, oblong, dark orange yellow, juicy and rich. One of the best yellow freestones.

III. Ripening June 20 to July 15.

Mountain Rose, large, round, white flesh, red cheek, free.

Pallas, large, flesh white, melting, with a rich vinous aroma, profuse annual bearer.

Gen. R. E. Lee, cling similar to Chinese Cling, but earlier and more prolific.

Early Belle, (new) very large, skin white, with red cheeks, flesh white, firm and of excellent flavor; tree a rapid grower and very prolific; a seedling of Chinese Cling.

Champion, very large peach, highly flavored and beautifully colored; flesh white and skin white with red cheek, small pit and thick flesh.

Crosby, medium, fine rich yellow color, with streaks and shades of carmine.

Hero, a splendid variety for canning purposes. The tree grows of very large size and produces beautifully colored, white fleshed, juicy, clingstone peaches in great abundance, sure to bear every year.

Belle of Georgia (new), very large, white freestone of excellent flavor. Trees grow and bear well; fruit a very good shipper.

IV. Ripening July 15 to August 10.

Carpenter's Cling, large, white, with a tinge of red, sweet, juicy, very productive.

Elberta, the peach that every one knows. A large yellow freestone, red next to pit. The peach for the market.

Old Mixon Free large, greenish white, with red cheek; flesh white, juicy and of good flavor. Ripening in July.

Comal Cling (new), the best, largest and finest yellow clingstone. The original tree was found growing behind an old house at one of my neighbors' 16 years ago. Fruit very large, dark yellow with dark red cheeks to the sunny side; flesh yellow, juicy and sweet; trees growing to a large size; leaves very large; a regular bearer. Ripens July 1 to 16.

Old Mixon Cling, the juiciest and best flavored white clingstone peach; of very large size and best bearing qualities.

Chilow, a large yellow peach, like Elberta, but a clingstone; originated near Austin; a good bearer and shipper.

Thurber. very large, white flesh, red cheek, sure productive.

Lemon Cling, large, yellow, sure bearer and highly flavored.

Indian Blood, large, dark claret with red veins, downy; flesh a deep red, very juicy, vinous and refreshing. August, clingstone.

Everbearing. Originator says: "The fruit begins to ripen about the 15th of July and continues to ripen until the 15th of September. Blooms at intervals, consequently no danger of frost killing entire crop of fruit." 25 cents each.

V. Ripening August 10 to September 1.

Snow Cling, one of the best peaches for canning; size medium, flesh clear, creamy white throughout; juicy, melting, sweet and sprightly flavor; enormous bearer.

Matthews' Beauty, a large, new, yellow peach of the Smock strain, but of extra good quality; very showy and a valuable shipper. 25 cents.

Indian Free, very productive and of excellent quality. One real good late peach.

Ward's Late, large, globular, white with red cheek, very good, prolific.

VI. Ripening September 1 to October 1.

Lemon Free, light yellow flesh, melting, a large late peach, prolific.

Caruth, yellow freestone, very prolific, hardy and good quality.

Stump the World, very large, white with bright cheek; flesh white, juicy and of good flavor. A fine market peach.

Heath White, large, oval with sharp apex; skin creamy white, juicy, sweet and good aroma. A very popular clingstone. September.

VII. Ripening into October.

October Indian, of medium size and with red cheek. Very hardy and good bearer.

Henrietta, the best late clingstone. Very large, yellow, crimson cheek; a regular bearer.

Wonderful, a remarkably fine yellow freestone.

Leopard, one of the latest peaches known. In 1889 I had fresh fruit at Christmas. Tree looks very healthy and is long lived. The fruit is large and round; flesh white and brittle.

November, this is the latest of all peaches, ripe in November; good freestone. Has been grown near New Braunfels for the last 50 years.

Common Seedlings, extra strong; 5 cents each, $4 per 100.

We have a large stock of June budded peach trees on hand, all of the leading varieties at the low price of 10 cents each or $8.00 per hundred. I can recommend these trees especially to large planters; they are well rooted, as a June budded peach tree has not yet lost its fibre roots. They are fast growers and can be easily grown into a shapely tree. As such stock is very light, the transportation charges are very low.

Plums.

In order of ripening.   4 to 6 feet, 20 cents each, $2.25 per 12, $18 per 100.
Extra large 2-year selected trees and some new plums, 25 cents each.
2 to 3 years, bearing age trees, well headed, 50 cents each, $5 per 12.

There is no fruit tree that bears such an abundance of fruit at so early an age as does the plum. Many varieties bear the first year after planting, and for this single reason should be most extensively planted. A plum tree requires very little care, but for the fact that it produces its fruit in such a great abundance the tree does not live very long and new trees ought to be planted every year to always have an abundance of this useful fruit. The American or Chickasaw varieties are mostly used for preserves and jellies, while the Japanese varieties are used for the table.

Rich loam with gravel subsoil is the best soil for plum culture, while sandy soil is almost as good if manured.

The following is the best collection for the South, and cannot be excelled by any:

Es giebt keinen anderen Obstbaum, der schon so jung nach dem Verpflanzen Früchte hervorbringt, als der Pflaumen=Baum. Von manchen Sorten sind schon einjährige Bäume mit Früchten beladen. Dieser Obstbaum sollte hier mehr angepflanzt werden, da er ja wenig Kultur verlangt und eine der dankbarsten Obstarten ist. Die amerikanischen Sorten eignen sich besonders gut zum Einkochen und die japanesischen sind als Tafel=Obst sehr beliebt. Da der Pflaumen=Baum in unserem Klima so überreich trägt, ist seine Lebensdauer kurz und sollte man jedes Jahr einige Bäume anpflanzen um immer gesunde, tragende Bäume zu haben. Reicher Lehmboden sagt den Pflaumen am besten zu. Folgende Auswahl von Sorten ist die allerbeste für den Süden und Westen und kann nicht übertroffen werden.

McCartney, new, of Texas, larger than Wild Goose, 14 days earlier, egg-shaped, golden yellow color, enormous bearer. This is the best yellow plum.

Mrs. Clifford, larger than Wild Goose, pear-shaped, red, meaty, with a fine pineapple flavor.

Transparent, one of the best yellow Chickasaw plums. Tree is very productive and sure every year. The fruit is so transparent that you can almost see the pit through the skin, and is very delicious.

Lone Star, tree grows very round and spreading and produces a beautiful shade tree. Bears red plums of medium to large size, which are very juicy and sweet.

Yellow Japan,one of the earliest Japanese plums. It is a heavy and regular bearer; color a clear yellow; fruit heart-shaped, of good size, very sweet and firm. Ripens end of May and beginning of June.

Excelsior,new, seedling of Kelsey Japan. Fruit medium, sweet, juicy, melting, color reddish purple; a good early plum.

Wild Goose,Chickasaw, vigorous, red, large, very good, abundant when fertilized.

Mikado,a very large plum of greenish yellow color, nearly round, very little suture, a rapid grower, more so than any other. This is the most remarkable of all plums for its enormous size, beauty and good quality. It is probably the largest plum in existence.

Mariana,vigorous, red, medium, good bearer, very fine for a shade tree. 15 cents each, $10 per 100; 6 to 7 feet, well branched, 25 cents each.

Sweet Botan Japanese, one of the finest older varieties, which is too popular to need long description.

Gonzales,a cross between the American and Japan plum. The fruit is as large as a large Botan, it is sweet and juicy and will keep a week after ripening. The tree is a good grower and is very prolific. It ripens the middle of June.

Climax,a cross of Simoni and Botan. Very large, and so fragrant a whole house is perfumed with a single fruit. Mr. Burbank says: "Productive as Burbank, several times as large, two or three weeks earlier and very much more nicely colored; the most wonderful plum ever grown and one that will change the whole business of early fruit shipping."

Shiro, a combination of Robinson, Myrobolan and Wickson. Rank grower, enormously productive, fruit will keep a month, and is so transparent the pit can be seen through the flesh; egg-shaped. Ripens two weeks before Burbank.

America,a seedling of Robinson, crossed with Botan. The most beautiful of all plum trees in appearance. It is of large size, a little above the average size of Japanese plums, and from four to sixteen times as large as the popular American varieties. Flesh of a light yellow color, moderately firm and very delicious. Ripens two or three weeks earlier than Burbank. Exceedingly prolific.

Red June,a vigorous, hardy, upright, spreading tree, productive, fruit medium, deep vermillion red, flesh light lemon yellow and of pleasant quality. Early.

Everbearing this is certainly a fine plum. The fruit is small, but deliciously flavored and very sweet, and is produced in great abundance. Should be gathered under the tree (not picked off) every morning. Begins to ripen about the middle of June and continues to about the middle of August, the last fruit being just as good as the first. 25 cents each.

Wassu this is a valuable new plum. The growth of the tree, size of fruit and productiveness are the same as in Burbank, but the fruit is much sweeter and has a fine flavor. Ripens a few days before Burbank.

Chalco a cross between Burbank and Simoni, the beautiful, fragrant Asiatic plum, and is the first one of the strain ever produced. The fruit, which ripens just before Burbank, is large, flat like a tomato, deep reddish purple, with very sweet, rather firm, exceedingly fragrant, yellow flesh and a small seed. The fruit completely surrounds the older branches as thick as it can stick, like kernels on a huge ear of corn. Good keeping quality.

OUR ONE-YEAR-OLD PLUM TREES

Burbank, Japanese, named after the introducer of this and most of the other good plums. The best bearing variety we have. When fully ripe, the fruit is deliciously sweet.

Normand's Japan, Japanese; beautiful golden color, larger than Burbank, apple shape, ripe end of June.

Hale, tree good grower, fruit very large, beautifully colored, of best quality, ripe August. Does well in poor soil.

Wickson, Japanese, tree grows in vase form, sturdy and upright. The fruit is evenly distributed all over the tree. It changes to white when about half grown and remains so until a few days before ripening, when it changes to a glowing carmine. Small stone, the flesh is of fine texture, firm, sugary and delicious, and will keep two weeks after ripening. A fine rare plum.

Bartlett, a cross between Simoni and Delaware. Said to have exactly the quality, flavor and fragrance of the Bartlett Pear, but the Bartlett Plum is so much superior to the pear, that no one will ever eat the pear if this plum is at hand. Fruit turns deep crimson when fully ripe. Light, salmon-colored flesh.

Satsuma, a very large and well flavored plum with blood-red flesh. Skin blueish red. Pit is very small. Tree grows very large and old, and is a very good bearer.

Robinson, tree spreading and round in shape. About the most productive of all. The fruit is of medium size and often colors up two weeks before it can be gathered. Has to be soft before edible. Robinson has stood droughts better than any other with me.

Kelsey's Japan, vigorous, greenish yellow, very large, excellent, prolific, sweetest of all plums, early bloomer.

Sultan, a cross between Wickson and Satsuma, and the flesh is wine or garnet colored like that of Satsuma. The fruit is of unusual size and of remarkable beauty of form and color, 1 and 2 year old trees 25 cts. each.

June Budded Plums, best varieties, at 12½ cents each or $10.00 per 100.

Mulberries.

6 to 8 feet, 25 cents each; $2.50 per 12.

As a shade tree for the chicken yard the mulberry is about the best tree to be had. Chickens eat the fruit as soon as it drops from the tree. The finer varieties are also eaten by children. The tree grows very quickly and is easily transplanted.

Als Schattenbaum und für den Hühnerhof kann der Maulbeerbaum nicht übertroffen werden, da die Hühner die Frucht gerne fressen. Kinder lieben die Früchte sehr. · Der Baum wächst schnell und ist leicht zu verpflanzen.

Hicks Everbearing, profuse, 3 months, fine grower for shade, and the best of all trees for the fowl yard.

Russian, unquestionably the best as a shade tree. The tree is very hardy and long lived, and grows rapidly to a beautiful round shape. The fruit is small and does not drop from the tree when ripe; some trees do not produce fruit at all. It is very much sought for street planting, for the shining leaves stand the dust well. 4 and 5 feet, 15 cents; 6 to 7 feet, 25 cents.

English, a very quick-growing mulberry, with very large and well shaped leaves. The fruit is very large and of black color. Stem is very straight and can be topped at almost any desired height.

Japan Persimmons.

(Diospyros Kaki.) A fruit from the orient that has come to stay. The growing of this fruit in the south, both for market and home consumption, is no longer an experiment. It has proven itself adapted to the whole cotton belt, and is becoming quite popular on the northern fruit markets.

Trees on the native persimmon will grow on any soil in the South, but are not long lived in wet, low places; high, well-drained, sandy soil suits them best, and they will do better on very poor land than any other kind of fruit tree. They are especially suited for planting in old peach orchards, as the old peach trees become worthless, or to replant the land after a peach orchard has been destroyed.

Fruit should be shipped just before it begins to soften, and directions how to eat it should be printed on wraps to be used with each fruit and dealers instructed to display only ripe fruit.

Price of JAPANESE PERSIMMONS ON NATIVE PERSIMMON ROOT, 35 cents each or $3.50 per 12.

Die japanesische Persimone ist die süßeste aller Früchte und erst im Herbst, nachdem sie einen kleinen Frost bekommen hat, genießbar. Der Baum wächst langsam und ist mehr strauchartig, trägt aber sehr jung und reichlich. Der Baum ist etwas schwierig umzupflanzen da er nur eine Pfahlwurzel hat, auch wird das Holz oft im Frühjahr nach der Steigung des Saftes durch Spätfröste getödtet.

Costata, medium, oblong, conical, pointed, somewhat four-sided, diameter 2¼ inches longitudinally, and 2⅜ inches transversely, color of skin salmon yellow, nearly seedless; astringent until ripe, and then very fine, one of the latest to ripen, and a good keeper; tree the most ornamental of all, it being a very rapid, upright grower, with large luxuriant foliage.

Dia Dia Maru, tree of rather open growth, with distinct light foliage, fruit medium size, shape flat like a tomato, slightly four-sided, flesh white, quality very fine.

Hachiya, very large, oblong, conical, with sharp point, very showy, diameter 3½ inches longitudinally and 3 inches transversely, color of skin reddish yellow, with occasional dark spots or blotches and rings of apex; flesh dark yellow, some seed, astringent until fully ripe, then very good. Tree vigorous and very shapely.

Hyakume, Large, to very large, varying from roundish oblong to roundish oblate, but always somewhat flattened at both ends, generally slightly depressed at the point opposite the stem, nearly always marked with rings and veins at the apex, skin light buffish yellow, flesh dark brown, sweet, crisp and meaty, not astringent, good while still hard, a good keeper, one of the best market sort. Tree of good growth and sure bearer.

Okame, large, roundish, oblate, always showing a peculiar corrugated appearance at the stem end, somewhat four-sided, flesh yellow with but few seeds, rich, meaty, free from astringency, quality fine, tree a good bearer.

Triumph, Origin near Sanford, in Orange county, Florida, from seed from Japan. Its quality is of the best, size medium, tomato-shaped, color of skin dark red, handsome and showy, flesh yellow with but few seeds. It is very productive, the fruit of a single tree having been sold for $17.00. Ripe in October and holds on the tree until January.

Tane-Nashi, very large, roundish, conical, pointed, very smooth and symmetrical, color of skin light yellow changing to bright red, at full maturity, flesh yellow, generally seedless, astringent until fully ripe, then one of the best.

Tsuru, longest in proportion to its size of all the varieties, slender, pointed, diameter 3¼ inches longitudinally and 2⅝ inches transversely, color of skin bright red, flesh orange colored, with dark coloring in immediate vicinity of seed, which are very few, very astringent until ripe, and one of the latest to ripen, a good keeper, and of good quality when full ripe. Tree a heavy bearer.

Yeddo-Ichi, large, oblate, very smooth in outline, with a slight depression at the end opposite the stem, color of skin a darker red than most varieties. The flesh is dark brown color, verging into purple, and is quite seedy. In quality it is one of the best, being exceedingly rich and sweet, and, like the Hyakume is good to eat while yet hard. Tree is heavy bearer and very thrifty.

Yemon, large flat tomato-shaped, somewhat four-sided, diameter 2¼ inches longitudinally and 3 inches transversely, very smooth and regular in outline, skin bright orange yellow, flesh yellow, generally seedless, quality very fine. Tree rather an open grower, with distinct foliage of a light shade.

Zengi, Although one of the smallest of the Japanese persimmons, it is the most valuable and reliable of them all. Roundish or roundish oblate, color reddish yellow. It is of the dark-meated class, being edible while quite hard, Can usually commence finding ripe fruit on the trees the latter part of August, and it continues to ripen until December, the trees hanging full of luscious fruit as late as Christmas. When allowed to remain on the tree until soft, it is excellent, being the sweetest and finest-flavored variety we have. Tree vigorous and reliable bearer, usually producing fruit the second year from planting. One of the most hardy varieties.

Pomegranates.

The pomegranate seems to have been created especially for our dry climate. It succeeds in any soil and bears regularly an abundance of the most refreshing fruit.

Little trouble is required for its culture. It is always free from all diseases, and grows in any deserted corner of the garden where no other fruit succeeds. The fruit is very sweet and refreshing, and ripens during August and September.

Der Granat = Apfel scheint speziell für unser heißes, trockenes Klima ge= schaffen zu sein, da er auch in der größten Dürre=Periode noch wächst ; auch ist er frei von jeder Krankheit und Ungeziefer. (Er trägt reich, die Früchte sind groß, wenn reif, sehr süß und von erfrischendem Wohlgeschmack. Reifezeit : August und September.

Old Favorite, is the best of all the fruiting pomegranates. I call it Old Favorite because it has been grown here at New Braunfels for at least 50 years, and it has proven to be far superior to all the other fruiting kinds which were introduced later. The fruit is the very largest, and refreshing and sweet. The tree or shrub is extremely hardy, and has glossy green leaves. Flowers are large and crimson in color. 25 cents each.

Grapes and Berry Plants.

•• •• ••

Grapes. Standard List.

In succession. Finest quality. This list contains the best and most successful. 10 cents each, $5 per 100, except where noted.

The grape thrives in almost any soil and is successfully grown all over
the South. With but little skill and labor it brings abundant crops every
year. The following are the best Southern varieties.

Die Weintraube gedeiht fast in jedem Boden und in jeder Gegend des Sü=
dens, mit etwas Mühe und Arbeit bringt sie reiche Früten. Folgende sind
gute Sorten :

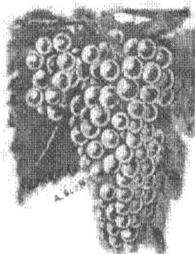

Early Ohio, said to be the earliest black grape.
Bunches large, compact and shouldered; berries of
medium size and adhere firmly to the stem; foliage
thick, leathery and healthy; very productive sort. 20
cents each.

Moore's Early, very large, black, good market.

Moore's Diamond, one of the finest American
grapes.

Lutie, berries large, beautiful lilac color,, of superior
flavor and unusually free from rot; a very desirable grape. 15 cents.

Worden, very large, black, good market; improved Concord.

Niagara, large, white, very good table and market grape.

Martha, large, white, table, market.

Concord, large, black, table, market.

Jacquez (Black Spanish, Le Noir, Blue French), small, large cluster,
black, red wine. 2 years, 10 cents, $8 per 100.

Herbemont (McKee, Bottsi, Brown French), small, large cluster, purple,
finest quality, table wine, best old grape in Southwest Texas. 10 cents, $8
per 100. Muscadine varieties, 25 cents each.

Scuppernong, clusters of two to six; berries large, round and of bronze
color; skin thin, free from rot. 25 cents each.

Thomsa bunches seldom exceed eight or ten berries; color reddish purple; pulp sweet, tender, vinous, quality equal or superior to any of the muscadine type. Ripens the middle of August. 25 cents each.

PEACHES   OUR THREE-YEAR-OLD ORCHARD   PLUMS

Eden, berry very large, black with delicate Thomas flavor; twelve to fifteen berries in a cluster; it is a profuse bearer, making an excellent brown wine resembling sherry. The Eden fills a long-felt want as a late table grape. 25 cents each.

Dewberries and Blackberries.

In Succession.

The blackberry is not so successfully cultivated in our part of the State as it is in North Texas, but the Mayes Dewberry reaches its greatest perfection here. It produces fruit of enormous size, of good flavor and in great abundance. Every lover of berries ought to have it.

Die Brombeere gedeiht hier nicht so gut wie im nördlichen Teras; aber die Thaubeere (Mayes Dewberry) erreicht hier ihre größte Vollkommenheit. Sie bringt erstaunlich reiche Ernten von riesengroßen Früchten. Jeder Beeren-Liebhaber sollte davon pflanzen.

Maye's Dewberry (like cut), new, very large, early, glossy black, highly flavored; it roots deep, is very prolific and never fails. Price, 50 cents per 12, $2.50 per 100.

White Dewberry, ripe 14 days before Mayes, a good, sweet berry. 50 cents per 12.

Dallas (blackberry), very vigorous, drooping, thorny, productive, large, fine. 50 cents per 12, $2.50 per 100, $15 per 1000.

Strawberries.

25 cents per 12, $1 per 100, $5 per 1000.

To grow strawberries with success irrigation is required in Western Texas, but where water may be had plentifully, it is very valuable, being about the first fruit in spring.

Die Erdbeere kann in West-Teras und anderen trockenen Gegenden nur mit Hülfe von Bewässerung gezogen werden, ist aber dann profitabel und das erste Obit, das reift.

Michel's Early, earliest of all; large, vigorous, perfect flower, a fine pollinator for other kinds.

Crescent, early, prolific, bright, excellent market, pistillate; needs Michel's Early to fertilize it.

Hoffman, an extra early berry for the South, very large and brilliantly colored.

Lady Thompson, very large, good shipper and prolific bearer; one of the best of the many varieties of strawberries.

Shade and Ornamental Trees.

.. .. ..

6 feet, 25 cents; 8 feet, 35 cents; 8 to 10 feet, 50 cents.
All shade trees are nursery grown, are straight and have splendid roots.

The physical welfare of yourself and those that you hold dear is greatly advantaged by the trees and plants which surround your home. What a deserted impression does a splendid house make if not a tree or plant is near, and what a pleasant feeling comes to you if you see a small hut surrounded by beautiful shade and ornamental trees. What a comfort does a single shade tree afford the farmer when, after he comes home from his toil in the field, he can recline under the same and take his afternoon nap.

Therefore, plant shade and ornamental trees around your house and you will be repaid for your trouble in many different ways.

Deine Zufriedenheit, Gesundheit und Wohlergehen liegt im Anpflanzen von Schatten- und Zierbäumen um Deine Wohnung und im Hofe. Was für einen öden und ungemüthlichen Eindruck macht das allerschönste Haus, wenn kein grüner Baum oder Strauch zu sehen ist; und was für einen einladenden und erfrischenden Eindruck macht schon die kleinste Hütte, wenn sie von Schattenbäumen umgeben und ein Zier- oder Blumengarten davor zu finden ist; deshalb pflanzt Schattenbäume, Ziersträucher und Blumen, ihr werdet reichlich belohnt durch den Genuß, welchen ihr daran findet.

Pyramidal Arbor Vitæ will make a large, fine evergreen shade tree, quick-growing, easily transplanted. Trimmed, with straight stem, 5 to 6 feet, 50 cents; 3 to 5 feet, 25 cents; untrimmed, 2 to 3 feet, 15 cents each.

Ligustrum Japonicum makes a splendid evergreen shade tree; leaves dark green, pointed, 2 by 2½ inches long; produces large bunches of creamy white flowers, followed in autumn by purple berries. Price of trees, well trimmed, 3 to 4 feet, 25 cents; 4 to 6 feet, 50 cents each.

Catalpa Japan Hy., a very pretty and extremely hardy, as well as ornamental shade tree. The leaves are 6-10 inches across; tree produces large clusters of very beautiful yellow flowers in spring. 6 to 8 feet, 25 cents, $2.50 per 12.

American Ash, a tree which is particularly well adapted to this latitude; makes quick growth and forms nice tops; leaves are of a lively green color. 6 foot trees, 25 cents each.

Cottonwood, a delightful, quick-growing shade tree. 4 to 6 feet, 15 cents; 6 to 8 feet, 25 cents each.

Liliodendron Tulipifera, Tulip Tree, one of the grandest of our native trees, of tall pyramidal growth, with broad, glossy, fiddle-shaped leaves and beautiful tuliplike flowers. 3 feet, 25 cents each.

ROBINIA.

The Robinia is one of our most ornamental shrubs or small trees and should be planted in every ornamental garden. The fine butterfly flowers in early spring are most ornamental. I have the five best varieties in cultivation, all grafted stock, as follows:

Heterophylla, foliage in various shapes, some leaves long, others rounded; flowers from medium to large, of creamy white color. Grafted, 50 cents each.

Rosea Grabra, tree of slow but compact growth, leaves large; has very few thorns, blooms in clusters and flowers are large; color shining pink. Grafted, 50 cents each.

Bessoniana, forms without trimming a nice rounded top, and is especially suited for planting along alleys or in parks; flowers light yellow. Grafted, 50 cents each.

Decaisneana tree of upright growth; color of flowers light pink, changing to white when open. Grafted, 50 cents each.

Semperflorens This is the richest bloomer; it blooms in early spring and in fall; color pure white and very fragrant. Grafted, 50 cents each.

Rhus Cotinus, Purple Fringe, a beautiful shrub, much admired for its long, feathery flower stalks, which gives the tree the appearance of being covered with a cloud of smoke. 25 cents each.

Rhus Coriaria, a very ornamental, quick growing tree. 25 cents each.

Sterculia Platanafolia (Japan Varnish Tree), a very hardy, and at the same time very beautiful shade tree. It is particularly adapted to this climate, but not very well known. The stem is always straight and smooth and has the same color as the leaves, which is a beautiful light green. The leaves are from 6 to 10 inches across. Tree produces a spreading and dense top and grows to very large size. A tree of fancy appearance, but stands as much drought as a hackberry. 3 to 5 feet, 50 cents; 6 to 8 feet, $1.00 each.

Salisburia, (Maidenhair Tree). A rare, elegant tree from Japan, with singular foliage, unlike that of any other tree. Foliage fern-like, grows to a good-sized tree, in every way desirable. 3 feet, 35 cents.

Sycamore, a lofty white spreading tree, heart-shaped leaves, valuable for its handsome foliage and free growth. 25 cents each.

Weeping Willow, a grand old tree for the cemetery and for the lawn. Should be planted in deep, rich soil, where it is constantly moist. 25 cents each.

Umbrella China, a native of Harris Co., and now widely known over the State. It is the finest and quickest-growing of all shade trees. I think I have the largest stock of them in Texas. 6 to 7 feet, branched, 35 cents; 5 to 6 feet, 25 cents; 3 to 5 feet, not branched, 15 cents each.

POPLARS.

Populus Alba, the white poplar. A quick-growing ornamental tree. 5 to 6 feet, 25 cents each.

Populus Bolleana, the pyramidal silver poplar. Does well here. 5 to 6 feet, 25 cents each.

Populus Nivea, Silver-leaved poplar. 5 to 6 feet, 25 cents each.

Popu us Pyramidalis, Italian poplar. A rapid-growing tree. 6 to 8 feet, 25 cents each.

All the poplars are easy to transplant and quick-growing.

Sbrubs.

All tested and successful in Texas.

All the following shrubs have been tested for years, and found to be especially adapted to the South. I have a splendid stock of fine plants for this year's trade.

Alle die folgenden find feit Jahren hier verfucht und als die beften für unfer Klima gefunden worden. Jch habe einen großen Borrath davon und ftarfe, fräftige Pflanzen.

ALTHEAS
GRAFTED ON HARDY STOCK.

One of the best hardy, flowering shrubs that we know of, and most especially adapted to West Texas, for the reason that it blooms during the entire summer, even then when monthly roses and other everblooming flowers are not in bloom. The flowers are not in the least affected by the hot sun in July and August, but are just as beautiful then as they are in the cooler months. Price of strong plants, 25 cents, $2.50 for 12; smaller 15 cents each.

Boule de Feu, pink flowers, double. 25 cents each.

Coelestis, sky blue color, double. 25 cents each.

Comte de Haynaut, flesh colored, double. 25 cents each.

Coerulea, very large, pink. 25 cents each.

Duke of Brabant, violet blue, single. 25 cents each.

Elegantissima, flesh colored, sometimes white, double. 25 cents each.

Fastuosa, very large, pink flowers with crimson stripes. 25 cents each.

Osmarante, 25 cents each.

Pulcherima, white, shading into pink, double. 25 cents each.

Souv. de Chas. Breton, large flowered, light blue, not very double. 35 cents each.

Variegata Plena, flesh color with red veins, double. 35 cents each.

Luteola Plena, large flowers of light yellow color, double. 35 cents each.

Speciosa Rubra, dark violet, single. 25 cents each.

Banner, double striped, white, pink and red, very beautiful sort.

Double Red Althea, the old double red, which produces the prettiest and largest flowers of all. It is one of the most desirable, and most profusely blooming. 20 cents each.

Leopoldll, very beautiful and rare kind, the color being pink and the flower double. 25 cents each.

Mechan's Double White, pure white flowers with large, fiery center.

Pompon Rogue, pretty double red flowers. 25 cents each.

Tota Alba, single, pure nearly white; dwarf habit; earliest of all Altheas to bloom, and bloom freely. Don't overlook this sort, because it is single, it is very desirable.

CRAPE MYRTLES.

The Crape Myrtle has reached such a high degree of popularity that there is hardly a flower garden without a few of these lovely flowering shrubs. They are lately being used for hedges, which produces the most striking effect, and such a hedge is admired by all who see it. The first flowers appear early in May, and from then until frost the plant is continuously a mass of flowers. Price of strong plants, 2 to 3 feet, 25 cents; 3 to 4 feet, 35 cents each.

Pink, the earliest of all Crape Myrtles to bloom. Tree is of a rather dwarfish habit, but produces more flowers in one season then any of the others.

Crimson, grows to a good sized tree and is almost always in bloom. The flowers are of a very rich crimson color.

Purple, the largest of all; produces very pretty purple flowers in great clusters.

White, always rare. The white Crape Myrtle is a very profuse bloomer but slow grower. 35 cents each.

Tartarian or Bush Honeysuckel, an upright growing honeysuckel, which has the same foliage as the climbing honeysuckel; and produces very pretty red flowers, which are followed by deep red berries. 25 cents each.

SYRINGA—Lilacs.
ALL GRAFTED STOCK EXTRA FINE.

Alba, large, pure white flowers, produced in large clusters. 25 cents each.

Charles X, purplish red flowers. Adapted to forcing. 35 cents each.

Emodi, very beautiful foliage; flowers pinkish white. 35 cents each.

Grandiflora, largest flowering we have, color pure white. 35 cents each.

Emodi Variegata, similar to Emodi, but foliage is fringed white. 35 cents each.

L. Spaeth, flowers very large and of a dark crimson color. 35 cents each.

Persia Blanche, of tall growth, long slender limbs, flowers white. 25 cents each.

Persia Rosea, growth same as above and flowers of rose color. 25 cents each.

Purpurea Marly, the purple-flowered variety of Marly. 35 cents each.

Purple Lilac, a well known favorite. 15 cents each.

SPIREA.

Spiræa Atrosanguinea, a very fine purple-flowered variety. 35 cents each.

Spiræa Paniculata Rosea, a beautiful rose colored variety. 35 cents each.

Spiræa Van Houttel, a splendid new garden shrub and one of the most beautiful of all. Immense bloomer of snow white flowers. 25 cents each.

Spiræa Prunifolia (Bridal Wreath), flowers white and double like little roses, borne in great profusion the whole length of the branches. 25 cents each.

New Japanese Blue Spiræa (Coryopteris Mastacanthus), this is a new hardy blue-flowering shrub, and very handsome and desirable in every way, makes a neat compact bush two feet high, begins to bloom in July or August and continues loaded with lovely sky-blue flowers till it freezes. Very sweet and the best blue-flowering garden shrub we know. Plants, two years old, extra strong, 35 cents each.

Broad=leaved Evergreens

These are easily transplanted and grow very rapidly; therefore, they should never be overlooked when ordering. You will always have a vacant place for a few. All the leaves should, however, be cut off before planting, otherwise they often fail to grow.

Folgendes find die allerbeiten Sorten und follten nicht überfehen werden. Sie find leicht und ficher zu verpflanzen, nur follte alles Laub beim Verpflanzen abgefchnitten werden, fonft vertrocknen fie häufig.

Buxus Arborea, or English Tree Box, succeeds almost everywhere. It is of rather slow growth compared with other evergreens, but remakable for its longevity, and finally gets to be 10 to 12 feet high. Strong bushes, 25 cents each; small plants for hedges, $10 per 100. The Buxus makes the finest evergreen hedge.

Japan Medlar, tree of medium height, with long, glossy leaves, which are evergreen, flowers white in spikes and produced in winter, fruit of the size of a wild goose plum, round or oblong, bright yellow, and produced in clusters, subacid and refreshing, maturity from end of February to April.

California Privet, splendid for specimens, screens or hedges. 2 to 3 feet, 10 cents; for hedging, $2.50 per 100. Have large stock.

Ligustrum Japonicum. This is the best of all privets, having dark green, pointed leaves, 2 to 2½ inches, fast growth, fine for hedges or single specimen. It produces large bunches of creamy white flowers. It is strictly evergreen, 25 cents each.

Ligustrum Japonicum Correaceum, a very thick-leaved, dark green variety. Grafted, 50 cents each.

Ligustrum Japonicum Lucidum, a fine bright green variety. Grafted, 50 cents each.

Ligustrum Japonicum Macrophyllum, a large bright-leaved variety. Grafted, 50 cents each.

English Holly, one of the most valuable broad-leaved evergreens, leaves richest glossy green, tree covered with bright red berries in fall. 25 cents each.

Magnolia Grandiflora, its large, shining, green foliage, accompanied in summer with large, fragrant, milky-white flowers, places it pre-eminently above all ornamental trees. This as well as all other evergreens should be handled and planted very carefully, as they are extremely sensitive to injury from drying. Their roots should never be allowed to get dry when out of the ground. In planting, the soil should be pressed firmly about the roots with the foot. Neither should they be planted with roots curled in shallow holes. 3 to 4 feet, 50 cents; 12 to 14 inches, 25 cents each.

Magnolia Acuminata, hardy, growth of a tree form, flowers greenish-yellow. 2 to 3 feet, 25 cents each.

Mahonia Aquifolia, (Holly-leaved), a distinct and beautiful evergreen shrub, with large, dark purplish green, prickly leaves, and showy bright yellow flowers in March and April. 50 cents each.

Euonymus Japonicus, one of the fastest growing evergreen shrubs, suitable for either hedge or single specimen; can be greatly improved by cutting back to induce bushy form. No evergreen has such a bright, dark green color in winter as this. For quick results this excels. Fine strong plants, 20 cents; $2 per 12. For hedges it is very fine, $10 per 100.

Euonymus Europæus, a most ornamental evergreen, very hardy and of upright growth; foliage dark green, longer and not so thick as that of Euonymus Jap. Straight trees, 2 to 3 feet, 50 cents each.

Pittosporum Tobira, the finest of all evergreen shrubs, well adapted for trimming, grows round and compact. 50 cents each.

LEUCOPHYLLUM TEXANUM.

A native of the dry regions of our state, where it is found growing among cliffs and rocks. It is a plant of rare beauty; in fact, one of the most beautiful shrubs in existence, but owing to the great difficulty of starting young plants, it has never been grown in nurseries. I have for many years tried to find some means of starting young plants in pots, and have now found a way of growing this plant. The young plants I herewith offer for the first time to my customers are in small pots, and will be sent with the pot, which is broken before setting. This is the only sure way of transplanting, and I guarantee every plant to grow which is thus treated.

The plant grows round and dense; attains height of six feet and same width. Foliage is a beautiful silvery gray color, which is, however, hidden when plant is in full bloom. The purplish red flowers are half an inch across, with golden dots on inside, and are produced in such numbers every two weeks that the plant looks from a distance as if loaded with ripe fruit. It is an evergreen as well as an everblooming plant. Stands drought better than any other shrub, but thrives in moist soil best.

Price of plants in four-inch pots (with pot), and guarantee that plant will grow, $1.50 each; field grown, 3 feet, $1.00 each.

Cone=bearing Evergreens.

We do not think we exagerate when we say that we have the largest stock of the cone-bearing evergreens in the State. We have in fact almost overstocked ourselves with them, and can afford to sell extra fine plants at a very low price. We grow all and only such varieties as succeed in Texas. Sizes are from 1 foot up to 7 feet, and the prices, as you will notice, are lower than those of any other nursery, taking in consideration the quality of the plants.

Ich glaube nicht zu viel zu jagen, wenn ich behaupte, dieses Jahr den größ= ten Vorrath und die feinsten Exemplare von immergrünen Nadelhölzern in Texas zu haben. Ich habe alle Arten, welche hier gedeihen und alle Größen von einem Fuß an bis zu sieben Fuß Höhe und wird mein Preis niedriger sein, als irgendwo anders für Waaren derselben Güte.

True Berckmans. Biota Aurae Nana, a new Golden Arbor Vitæ of a dwarf and compact habit, perfect gem for small gardens or cemetery lots, will not grow higher than 6 to 8 feet. 12 to 15 inches high, 50 cents; 15 to 18 inches, 75 cents each.

Golden Arbor Vitæ, this is the handsomest and most compact of the Arbor Vitæs, green with a beautiful golden tint. True grafted trees, 2 to 4 feet, 50 cents each.

Pyramidal Arbor Vitæ, 4 to 5 feet, 50 cents; 1 to 2 feet, 15 cents.

Chinese Arbor Vitæ, dark green, vigorous, hardy, desirable. 3 to 5 feet, 25 cents each.

Golden Pyramidalis Arbor Vitæ, like the Golden, but grows tall and slender. A very ornamental sort. Do not confuse this with Cupressus Pyra-midalis. Three feet, 50 cents each

Rosedale Arbor Vitæ, very compact growth, with the sugar loaf form of the Golden Arbor Vitæ, but with fine, cedar-like foliage of a bluish cast. Makes a beautiful ornament; perfectly hardy and of vigorous growth; the most beautiful of all Arbor Vitæs. Two to three feet, 50 cents; extra large, fine plants, 75 cents each.

Compacta Arbor Vitæ, a compact growing Arbor Vitæ, of a lively dark green color and of globular shape. Two to four feet, 50 cents.

Cedrus Deodora, this is the great cedar of the Himalayas. It succeeds anywhere in the South, and attains a great size and age; the short needles are a bluish green; has a fine form and grows moderately fast. Two years, 50 cents each.

Red Cedar, one of the finest evergreens, which grows on almost any soil, and which requires much less water and care than the Arbor Vitæ. Will ac-quire any particular shape or size if properly trimmed. Trimmed to pyra-midal (or conical) form, 2 to 4 feet, 50 cents each.

Cupressus Pyramidalis. This is a beautiful, tall, columnar evergreen, does well in Texas, a little tender in far north. Three to four feet, 50 cents each.

Cupressus Horizontalis, like above, of rapid growth, but branches spreading. Two to three feet, 25 cents; three to four feet, 50 cents each.

Lawson Cypress, a rare evergreen from California; one of the most graceful; elegant drooping branches; hardy in the South. Two years, 50 cents each.

Strong field grown, 1 year, 25 cents each, $2.50 per doz., except where other-wise noted; 2 year old, extra strong, 35 cents each, $3.50 per doz.

Of all the flowers which man has taken in his care the rose has reached the highest degree of popularity. She is the queen of flowers, the flower of the poets, and will always be the dearest of flowers to the lovers of the beautiful.

While wild roses are met with in almost every country, the cultivation of the rose began probably at the same time when the civilization of man be-gan, and with the cultivation of man that of the rose has kept pace, being now at the same height of development as is humanity.

Of the many thousands of varieties which have for centuries been intro-duced by the hybridizers those of each succeeding century show a marked improvement over those of the foregoing. Of the roses which were consid-ered the best only a century ago only very few are grown today.

Many hundreds of different varieties have been tried on our grounds, and of all only such are described in the following list which in our judgment are the very best for outdoor planting.

Fortunately we live in a climate where even the tender roses stand the winter without cover, and any of the roses in this catalogue may be planted outdoors.

Plant your roses in an open place, never try to grow roses in the shade of trees. The plants you receive from us are grown by the latest methods of cultivation, which we practice together with a means of accumulating power and strength in the young plants, and which is just the opposite from forcing roses in greenhouses for bloom. Do not set out your roses the way you get them, but trim off at least one-half of the wood. Slow-growing sorts should be trimmed more severely than the quick-growing varieties.

Mein Vorrath an Rosen ist der größte in Texas und die Auswahl der Sor-sen ist die reichste.

Meine Rosen sind starke, im freien Felde gewachsene Büsche, die den ganzen Sommer hindurch geblüht haben und sind ja nicht mit den im Norden in Treibhäusern gezogenen, fingerlangen Topf = Pflanzen zu verwechseln. Diese Rosen, welche ich hier offerire, werden von Anderen zu 50 bis 75 Cents ange-boten. Folgende Liste enthält die besten und allerfeinsten Rosen, welche es giebt und kann keine bessere Auswahl getroffen werden :

CRIMSON AND RED.

American Beauty, hardy rose, of largest size, having the everblooming qualities of the tea rose, with the delicious odor of the Damask or Moss Rose.

In color it is a brilliant red, shading to a rich carmine crimson. The flowers are borne on long, stiff stems, hence a splendid rose for cutting. 2-year, extra large, 50 cents each.

Baron Girod, the color is varying shades of red, crimson and bright carmine; petals notched and flaked with white, like a Bizarre carnation. 50 cents each.

Baldwin, a new Hybrid Tea rose. About the best crimson outdoor bedding rose we now have. It is very strong-growing and healthy, and produces very large and double roses of a glowing carmine color, which are as sweet as a June Rose. 35 cents each.

The Burbank, raised by Mr. Luther Burbank, of California, known the world over as the "Wizard of Horticulture." The color is cherry-crimson; it is, in other words, the very deepest and brightest pink rose in cultivation. One of the freest bloomers and perfectly hardy.

Dr. Cazeneuve, flowers large, nicely formed; dark velvety crimson in color, like Jean Liaubaud; one of the finest of dark hybrid teas. 35 cents each.

Eli Lambert, the firm who sent us the first plants of this rose wrote us as follows: "We want your opinion later on Eli Lambert. It is a new H. P. and we think the grandest red of this section that our eyes have ever seen." This is what we wrote them later, and which we wish to repeat to our customers: "The Eli Lambert is simply grand. The color is so rich and lively that from a distance we can easily locate this rose in the field of red roses." 50 cents each.

Empress Alexandria of Russia, tea; an exquisite rose of a new shade of color; buds bronzy salmon, open flowers, lake red, shaded orange and crimson; of vigorous growth and very free in bloom. 50 cents each.

Gruss an Teplitz, we unhesitatingly say that for bedding, no rose we offer will compare with Gruss an Teplitz." It is a perfect sheet of rich crimson-scarlet all summer. When we say that we know of no rose that has such bright colors in it as this variety, we are stating facts. The nearest we can describe is that it is the richest velvety crimson overlaid with the brightest penetrating scarlet. 35 cents each.

Jean Liaubaud (Hy. Perpetual), this is the darkest rose among all the crimsons.

Jubilee, stands pre-eminently in the lead of the many dark Hybrid Perpetuals. In it are combined all the qualities that make a perfect rose; vigorous growth, perfectly formed flowers and great freedom of bloom. 50 cents each.

Liberty, pronounced the greatest crimson scarlet rose ever introduced. A grand new Hybrid Tea, of the color and character of General Jacqueminot. Most nearly approached by Meteor in color, but far surpassing that excellent variety in brilliancy and purity of color, as well as in size and freedom in bloom.

Madame Charles Wood, a true perpetual bloomer. The flowers are extra large, very double and full and quite fragrant. Color is a bright fiery scarlet, passing to fine, rosy crimson, elegantly shaded with maroon.

Meteor, a velvety red ever-bloomer of the deepest glowing crimson, as fine as a Hybrid. Flowers very double and petals slightly recurving. A beautiful open rose.

Red Captain Christy, the flowers are of magnificent form, very double, and stand erect in their material bearing. The color is a deep and beautiful red; in fact, it is often spoken of as the ideal red rose. Received compliments from the most critical flower lovers. 50 cents each.

Souv. D'Andre Raffy, one of the most beautiful of recent H. P. roses and very free in bloom, The flower is large, globular and full; color velvety crimson; form, freedom and color are all extra fine. 50 cents each.

PINK.

Bridesmaid, the pink sport of Catherine Mermet. It is a stronger grower than its parent, has handsome foliage, and the flowers are a much livelier pink. The most popular pink rose ever introduced.

Clara Watson, a beautiful rose of large size, very fragrant and fine form; color salmon pink, blended with blush pink on outer edge of petals, shading to yellow in center. Strong grower and profuse bloomer.

Champion of the World, a remarkable new sort, which combines the most desirable qualities. It is a perpetual bloomer, summer and winter. The flowers, which are produced in the greatest profusion, are perfectly double and of perfect shape; they are of a deep rosy pink and delightfully fragrant.

Duchess de Brabant, this rose never fails to produce flowers beautiful in open bud and open flower and a beautiful shade of soft, rosy flesh, deepening to warm pink and bright rose.

Duchess of Albany, red La France; very large, deep pink, full and highly perfumed.

Hermosa, the best pink bedder. The freest and most perpetual bloomer in existence.

J. B. M. Camm, a Hybrid Bourbon rose with very large foliage, bloom very large, extremely full of petals, always showing a pointed center; color a soft pink. A fine outdoor rose.

La France. Perhaps no rose is better known or more highly valued for a garden rose than La France. It is a Hybrid Tea, very beautiful form and color; an early and constant bloomer, producing a wonderful profusion of buds and flowers all through the growing season. It is exceedingly sweet and handsome, and altogether one of the loveliest and most desirable roses one can plant. The color is a delicate shade of peach blossom, changing to amber rose, elegantly tinged with crimson.

Mad. Abel Chatenay another rose of recent introduction which is bound to become very popular. The flowers are produced on long, stout stems. The color is a carmine rose, shaded salmon. 35 cents each.

Malmaison. This is certainly one of the choicest, and as a rose for general cultivation unsurpassed. The color is a beautiful rich, creamy flesh, with a rose center; flowers very large, perfectly double and deliciously fragrant; a strictly first-class rose in every respect.

M. Bunel, flowers large, composed of very large outer petals, diminishing towards the center; the open rose is of beautiful form, imbricated, and of rosy peach color, shading to pale gold, bordered with bright rose.

Mme. Eli Lambert. The flowers are extra large, very full and double; color is a rich pink on outside petals, as well as on tips of inside petals; the rest of the petals are white, gradually changing to yellow at the base of petals. A vigorous and healthy grower.

Mrs. Mawley, bright pink, shaded to salmon; very large and full; long plump buds on very long growths. A fine garden rose of magnificent size and build, free in growth. Nothing finer and better has yet been introduced,

Mrs. B. R. Cannt (new), a fine garden variety of even salmon shade; rose round and full, the form of a good H. P. A very free grower and free bloomer. It flowers as freely and continually as a China rose. It is especially fine in autumn. 40 cents each.

Mme. Mina Barbanson (new H. T.), this rose is very beautiful, its strong branching habit being admirable; each side shoot brings a perfect flower on a stiff stem; never shows a weak neck. The upper surface of each petal is shell pink, the reverse soft rose, very free and fragrant. 40 cents each.

Paul Neyron, deep pink, very large, and extra fine rose and very free bloomer. A rose without thornes.

Princess di Napoli, bright rosey flesh, color shading to pale pink, very fragrant and one of the freest in bloom. A fine grower, with brilliant dark foliage. 35 cents each.

Primula (Polyantha), a new showy, low-growing little bush, completely covered with cup shaped flowers, semi-double which are china roses at the edges and snow white in the center.

The arrangement of the color reminds one of the China primm rose. A pretty bedding plant. 50 cents each.

Queen of Edgley (Pink American Beauty), practically same as American Beauty, only difference is in color, which is a lovely pink, while the old American Beauty is red. It produces the same grand flowers on the same stiff and long stems, always in bloom and exquisitely fragrant. No further description needed. The fact that it is a pink American Beauty will sell more plants than we can grow. 50 cents each.

Souvenir de Jeanne Cabaud, a beautiful rose of most exquisite color. It is very large and very full, and its chief beauty is in its open state, when its appearance is that of a pink rose set in a yellow one. 35 cents each. I have a large stock of this rose.

Souvenir d'un Ami, a splendid tea rose; free flowering and vigorous in growth; color deep rosy flesh, beautifully shaded with rich carmine. Extra large globular form.

President Carnot. The flowers are large, full and double, exquisitely shaped, with heavy, thick, well-shaped petals. The buds are wonderfully beautiful long and pointed like Niphetos perfection in every line. The color is a new, delicate rosy blush, shaded a trifle deep at center of flower. Fragrance delicious; strong grower and free bloomer.

Vick's Caprice, a beautiful striped rose, perfectly hardy; color bright, rose distinctly striped deep carmine or crimson. On Manetti only, 35 cents each.

YELLOW.

Alliance Franco Russe (Tea), flowers bright yellow, shading to salmon at the center; bright and pleasing; has a strong upright stem and long bud; vigorous and hardy, and a free and continuous bloomer. Very full and double. 40 cents each.

Etoile de Lyon, many new varieties of yellow roses have been introduced since this was a novelty, but none combine more good qualities than this grand old sulphur-yellow rose. Buds are of beautiful shape and flower is very full.

Franz Deegen (Seedling of Kaiserin), this beautiful Hy. Tea rose is a fine grower, having dark leathery foliage and the good habit of throwing up numerous heavy canes, each one crowned by a glorious flower of large size, composed of large petals; the outer petals are of about the color of Perle, the inner petals a good orange shade, very deep and rich. It is a constant bloomer, opening its buds freely; a strong, healthy grower, not subject to mildew. $1.00 each.

Franciska Krueger, a strikingly distinct and handsome rose. One of the very best for open culture. The flowers are deeply shaded copper yellow in color, and are of large size. Always in bloom.

Golden Gate, a strong-growing rose, with long pointed buds of the same form as Nephitos. Color is a deep salmon, flushed with pink.

Helene Gambrier, this lovely, coppery-yellow, Hy. Tea, everblooming rose will fill a long-felt want from the fact that everybody has been looking and longing for a good yellow rose that combines vigorous hardiness with rich color and free blooming qualities. This Helene Gambrier does. Flowers are of a delightful shade of deep, rich coppery-yellow. 35 cents each.

Johanna Wesselhoft, another new rose found to possess great merit. It is considered the finest yellow rose for bedding. A beautiful canary yellow, and known as bedding Perle.

Lady Dorothy, a sport of Perle; very similar in color to Sunset, being a lovely mingling of pink and tawny buff.

Lady Mary Corry, a vigorous and erect-growing tea rose. Blooms are of good size, freely produced and of perfect form. Color deep golden yellow; distinct and fine.

Rosella, strong but compact grower; foliage shining green; flowers of good size, borne in great clusters; very double; color white, shading to clear yellow.

Perle des Jardins, golden yellow; large, double, free bloomer; the finest yellow rose in cultivation.

Soleil d'Or. For years have both American and European hybridizers tried to produce a rose like the Persian Yellow, but ever-blooming, and it was only very recently that the famous French rose grower, Pierre Ducher, claimed to have at last succeeded in producing the rose of our fancies. We at once imported at great expense a few sample plants of this rose, and are delighted to state that while Soleil d'Or is not a continuous sheet of deep yellow flowers, yet it is in the true sense of the word, "Ever-blooming Persian Yellow."

The flower is perfection in form, with conical buds, expanding into a large, full and globular flower, with incurved inner petals. The buds are a marvelous shade of rich chrome-yellow, with just a tinting of coppery rose in the center. The fully expanded flower is beautiful in its blendings of orange-yellow and gold, and nasturtium red, forming a color impossible to satisfactorily describe. 75 cents each.

Sunrise, has a long and very beautiful bud, but is equally beautiful when fully open. The color cannot be called yellow, but it is nearer yellow than anything else. The inside of the petals is yellow and the outside copper-colored. It shows great freedom of bloom here, and the plants are very healthy and quick growing. 35 cents each.

Sunset, a well known tea rose of large size, double, fragrant, and in color a most remarkable shade of rich golden amber, elegantly tinged and shaded with dark ruddy copper. Great bloomer.

WHITE.

Coquette de Alps, a lovely, pure white rose. Very full and free in flower. Erect growth and delicious fragrance.

Clothilde Soupert, profusely blooming perfect little rose of pearl white color with beautiful pink center. The flower is very double and lasts long.

Ivory, this is the white golden gate. Its extraordinary freedom, large size, heavy canes, all tend to make it a valuable white variety.

Kaiserin Augusta Victoria. This is one of the grandest of all roses. It is a strong, vigorous grower, producing buds and flowers of enormous size. Color pure ivory white. We have no hesitancy in saying that this rose is unequalled by any other in its color. A grand garden rose on account of its vigorous growth and hardiness.

Lady Clanmorris, a new British rose of perfectly distinct character. A splendid rose of very robust growth and free-branching habit, flowering continuously; blooms very large and of good form, creamy white with delicate salmon center, edge of petals margined pink. 40 cents each.

Marie Guillot, moderate grower, white, large, very full, none finer.

Mrs. Oliver Amis, this delightful new rose is round and full, with shell-shaped petals, recurving and ruffled at the edges. The color is creamy white, laced and shaded in pink. Foliage small, closely set, leathery and dark. 35 cents each.

Mme. Adophe Dahair (tea), new, flower large and full, borne on a very strong upright stem, satin white, shaded to cream, very free and odorous. 40 cents each.

Rosomane Gravereaux, this variety is of the general style of President Carnot, with an enormously long bud, producing a very large, very double, open flower, carried on a long stiff stem. The petals are very large; color silvery white, with reverse of rosy flesh; fragrant and free. 40 cents each.

Saxonia, an improvement of golden gate, and like it a strong grower and great producer of canes, the color is white, edged bright rose, quite distinct. This variety is well worth a trial. 50 cents each.

Snow Flake, one of the most beautiful white roses I have ever grown. The flowers are not very large, but always open to perfection. A very quick growing variety, and one that produces a tremendous amount of flowers the year round.

The Bride. This is decidedly the most beautiful white Tea Rose. It is a sprout from Catherine Mermet, with which it is identical in growth and shape of flowers. The flowers are very large and double, on long, stiff stems, of fine texture and substance, and last a long time after being cut. Makes one of the best varieties for corsage wear or bouquets. During extremely hot weather it becomes a pinkish white, at other times a beautiful pure white.

The Queen, a most charming tea rose, of pure, snowy white. The flowers are very beautiful in form and always open up fully. Has fine formed buds and is exquisitely sweet.

White Lady one of the startling new roses of recent date. It has gigantic flowers with enormous magnolia-like petals, one of the handsomest and most effective of all roses, and very distinct. The color is white, delicately flushed with pale pink, blooms are borne in great profusion on stiff stems, with heavy foliage. Longer stems would rank this with American Beauty, but we recommend it to every rose lover for trial. In England, the past year, it took the first place at Crystal palace show for twelve blooms of any white rose over theBride, Bessie Brown and others. 75 cents each.

White la France, pure white, large flowers, free bloomer, strong grower.

CLIMBERS.

Climbing Kaiserin Auguste Victoria, flowers same as the Kaiserin, which is too generally known to require description here. Stout canes, very quickly covers verandas, etc. Always in bloom.

Climbing Paul Neyron, a grand, new rose. Paul Neyron has always been known as the largest rose extant. In climbing Paul Neyron we have this large size, coupled with its bright, fresh, pink color in which that rose excels; and it is also a true perpetual bloomer.

Climbing Malmaison. This rose is the exact counter part in foliage and flower of the old Suv. de Malmaison, but it is a rampant climber. See description of Suv. de Malmaison.

Climbing Meteor is of strong, vigorous habit of growth, producing in great profusion throughout the season magnificently formed buds and flowers which in color are of a dark velvety crimson, the equal of any rose in cultivation, and possibly more glowing than its illustrious parent.

Climbing Perle des Jardins, a sprout from Perle des Jardins, the most popular of all yellow tea roses. Climbing Perle is a strong, vigorous, climbing Tea, with beautiful, large, double golden-yellow, flowers; larger and brighter than Perle.

Climbing Soupert, Clothilde Soupert is one of the most popular roses grown, filling a place all its own, and for which there is no substitute. The climbing Soupert has the same free vigorous habit and strong constitution; it is extremely hardy, withstanding zero weather and producing its fine clusters in profusion. This promises to prove the most valuable climbing sprout of any ever-blooming rose. 50 cents each.

Cloth of Gold, clear golden yellow, large, very full, and double, highly fragrant, a very fine climbing rose.

Estella Pradel, one of the freest bloomers we have. The buds are very fine and of the purest white, the open flower has a light yellow center.

James Sprunt, deep cherry red, flowers of medium size, very double and sweet. A strong, free-grower and very abundant in bloom.

La Marque purest white, a splendid climber and the freest and finest for winter blooming; has to be trimmed and trained well.

Marechal Niel, beautiful deep yellow, very large, full, globular form, sweet, free bloomer; the finest climbing rose. Budded upon Manetti, 35 cents, own roots, 25 cents each.

Mary Washington, a hardy, perpetual-blooming climber, producing large, double, snow white blossoms in great profusion from spring until frost. It is a sweet and most valuable sort.

Pink Perle, a splendid variety, with double pearl pink blooms, when open crimson in bud; foliage leathery and glossy, and very nearly evergreen. The finest wichuraiana Hy. yet produced. 40 cents each.

Philadelphia Rambler. This differs from the crimson rambler in three important points. The color is deep and more intense, the flowers are perfectly double to the center, very durable and of fine substance. The blooms are almost entirely free from the faded look often found in crimson rambler. It is very free in both growth and bloom, and will be found a splendid addition to the crimson rambler section. 75 cents each.

Reine Maria Henrietta, a strong-growing climber, making a great pillar rose. Flowers full and well formed; rich, brilliant crimson. A fine companion of Marechal Niel.

William Allen Richardson. The coloring of this rose is simply exquisite The base and back of petals are a bright yellow, the center highly colored with glowing copper and rose, first-class climber.

POLYANTHA OR FAIRY ROSES.

Mignonette, a lovely Fairy Rose, full, regular flowers, perfectly double and deliciously perfumed. Color, a clear pink, passing to white, tinged with pale rose.

Mademoiselle A. E. Nolte, flowers small, full, of perfect form. Color, deep yellow, passing to rosy-white. A true "Fairy Rose."

Miniature. This is the smallest of all roses, but of perfect form, regular, compact, fairy-like flowers, fully double and very fragrant. The color is creamy-rose, flushed with a peach-red.

Paquerette. We consider this variety the best of all the Polyantha Roses. The flowers are pure white, about 1 inch in diameter, and appear in clusters of from five to fifty blossoms.

Perle d'Or, charming and very distinct. Color a coppery-gold, changing to fawn and salmon, flat-rayed form and very double and elegantly perfumed.

Climbing, Clinging and Creeping Plants.

These long-lived plants are the most popular and best for the South to cover arbors, galleries, old trees, etc. in a very short time.

Diese ausdauernden Kletter = Pflanzen find die beliebtesten und besten für den Süden und eignen sich besonders für Lauben, Verandas und für Ueber= ranken von alten Bäumen, Zäunen 2c.

Antigonum Leptophus (Queen's Wreath), a splendid plant from Central Mexico, producing rose-colored flowers in racines two feet long. The profusion of bloom is such as to give the resemblance of roses at a distance, hence its name, "Rosa de Montana," or Mountain Rose. Will live out in the winter anywhere in the South. The vines are killed by frost, but it quickly shoots up in the spring and develops its flowers from May until frost. This is one of the most lovely vines. 25 cents each.

Ampelopsis Veitchii, (Boston Ivy), this plant resembles very much our ivy, but grows very rapidly, covering a large wall in one season. The foliage is small, neat, and blood-red color in fall. 25 cents each.

Hedera Denta, dentate-leaved ivy. 25 cents each.

Hedera Hibernica (Irish Ivy). 20 cents each.

Trumpet Creeper, a clinging vine of rampant growth; clings to wood or stone, walls or trees; very hardy; produces clusters of long trumpet-shaped, orange-scarlet flowers from early spring to late fall. 15 cents each.

HONEYSUCKLES.

Evergreen, the quickest-growing of all. It produces very large bunches of flowers, which open white and turn deep yellow. A bunch looks as if it was composed of flowers from two different plants. Extra large, 25 cents, smaller, 15 cents each.

Halleana, pure white, very large flowers and dense foliage. A desirable kind. 25 cents each.

Fuchsia Flowered, a new perpetual-flowering, weeping Honeysuckle. Its flowers are long and trumpet-shaped, beautiful coral red, borne in large clusters and droping like a Fuchsia. It is a strong, rapid grower, with beautiful leaves. 25 cents each.

Japan Golden Honeysuckle, a beautiful evergreen vine with a dark-green foliage, netted and mottled with gold, flowers white and very desirable. The leaves change to dark-green and purple in winter. 25 cents each.

Chinese Matrimony Vine, when trained, is a most vigorous and desirable hardy climber. It sends out numerous side branches, so that it covers a great space in a short time, and every new vine is at once covered with bright purple flowers, which are succeeded by brilliant scarlet berries nearly an inch long. The contrast between the dark-green foliage and shining scarlet fruit is beautiful. 15 cents each.

Clematis Paniculata, one of the most beautiful of our hardy climbing vines. The flowers are pure white, and are bone in great panicles or clusters of bloom, fairly cover the plant so that it is a mass or sheet of fleecy white. The fragrance is delicious, resembling the English Hawthorne Blossoms, and so subtle and penetrating that a large plant in bloom fills the air with exquisite fragrance. 25 cents each.

Clematis Vitalba, a strong, rampant grower, is very hardy, blooms white. 25 cents each.

Clematis Flamula, a vigorous grower, blooms profusely, large, pure white flowers. 25 cents each.

Clematis Viticella, a splendid variety of the utmost profusion of blooms, flowers of medium size and of bright wine-red color. A strong, free grower. 35 cents each.

Polygonum Multiflorum, splendid, fast-growing in the South, evergreen, rich flowering, white grapes. 25 cents each.

Phaseolus Caracella, curiously twisted, varied colored, large flowers. Highly interesting. 25 cents each.

Vinca Harrisemii, (trailing), two shades of green and gold, strong plants. 15 cents each, $1.50 per dozen.

Vinca Evergreen (trailing), dark-green. 15 cents each, $1.50 per dozen.

Wisteria Sinensis (Chinese Wisteria), a quick-growing climber, producing long racemes of purple flowers. 25 cents each.

Wisteria Frutescens (American Wisteria), a vine which covers porch in very short time and is covered in spring with large clusters of blue flowers. 25 cents each.

Wisteria (Sinensis Purpurea), flowers in clusters, pale blue, blooms in spring and fall. Strong two-year-plants, 25 cents each.

Wisteria (Sinensis Alba), flowers borne in long, drooping clusters of pure white color, very elegant. Strong two-year-plants, 40 cents each.

Ornamental Grasses.

No garden is complete without a few of these beautiful grasses. They are so easily transplanted and grow with so little care, that everybody can afford to have them. The beautiful plumes they produce keep for years, if cut at the right time and properly dried.

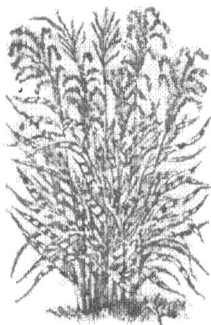

Kein Garten ist vollständig, in welchem diese schönen Ziergräser fehlen und da sie so leicht zu verpflanzen sind und fast gar keine Pflege beanspruchen, so sollte ein Jeder einige pflanzen, da ja auch die Blüthen so beliebt für Sträuße und Vasen sind und wenn gut getrocknet, Jahre lang halten.

Eulalia Japonica Zebrina. (Zebra Grass), bright green blades with white bars across them, grows to a height of five to six feet, produces fine, lace-like plumes which last for years if cut when fresh. Perfectly hardy. 15 cents each.

Eulalia Japonica Variegata, a variegated hardy grass from Japan. In appearance it somewhat resembles the Ribbon Grass while in a young state. It forms compact clumps, six feet in diameter; its flower stalks are very graceful and numerous. 15 cents each.

Eulalia Univittatae, very hardy and graceful, with elegant little plumes, 2 or 3 feet. 15 cents each.

Gynerium Argenteum (Pampas Grass), enormous bunches of long, handsome, dark-green blades, producing long stalks of silver-white plumes, 5 to 6 feet. 25 cents each.

Gynerium Elegans, plumes silvery white, produced upon very long stems; blooms early, a graceful new variety, 4 to 5 feet. 25 cents each.

Lemon Grass, came from Malabar, where, as in many other parts of the world, the tea made from it is a favorite beverage. A delightful perfume is extracted from the leaves. Highly valued for its medicinal properties and sweet fragrance, height 4 to 5 feet, large clumps. 25 cents each.

Gy. Roi des Roses, plumes very compact, of delicate rose color, very fine blooming and compact growing. New variety, 5 to 6 feet. 25 cents each.

Palms.

•• ••

Washingtonia Filifera, the palm which is planted out in the yard, where it will develop into a very large and fine specimen plant. It is the hardiest palm known, and there is no danger of its being killed by frost here. One-year-old plants, 25 cents each.

Sabal Palmetto This palm grows to be a large tree and is planted outdoors in our latitude. Fine specimens are found in the park surrounding the San Antonio City Hall. Two-year-old plants, 50 cents each.

Cannas.

Dry, divided roots, the best to transplant, 15 cents each; $1.50 per 12.

This is one of the most thankful of flowers. It produces its flowers from spring until the frost kills the top of the plant, and in such different and exquisite colors that nobody can help admiring them. The plant needs plenty of watering, and can only be had where there is a plentiful supply of same.

Dieſes iſt eine der dankbarſten Blumen, da ſie vom Frühjahr bis zum Herbſt, wenn der Froſt ihren Wuchs endet, blüht und zwar in ſolch friſchen, leuchtenden Farben, daß einem ein blühendes Can= na = Beet große Freude bereitet. Dieſe Pflanze ge= braucht viel Waſſer und kann nur dort gezogen wer= den, wo ſolches zur Verfügung ſteht.

Alphonse Bouvier. In color this is the most intensely brilliant crimson yet introduced, and it is undoubtedly the best bedding variety for planting in masses. The foliage is rich green; the plant is of strong, robust habit.

Austria (new), the gorgeous new orchid-flowered canna, a hybrid with "Canna Flaccida" as one parent; flowers of immense size, 5 to 6 inches across. Color, golden yellow.

Burbank (new). The flowers are of immense size, spreading fully seven inches. Form is semi-double. Color, a rich canary-yellow, with spots of deep, fine crimson toward the inner part of the lower petals. The leaves are of rich green, somewhat of the appearance of large rubber-tree leaves.

Betsy Ross, a good pink variety, with rounded and overlapping petals. It is of moderate size, but perfect form, and the truss is compact and well filled; the best pink canna to date. 25 cents each.

Chicago, Clear vermilion scarlet, flowers large and nearly flat, forming large heads of bloom. 20 cents each.

Gov. Roosevelt, an entirely new and distinct variety. It is a "sprout" from a scarlet-flowered sort, and instead of being mottled or spotted like all other variegated sorts, it is striped bold and strong like a camelia. In some petals the coloring matter runs in even bands of red and yellow, others on the same stem will be all red, some flowers will be entirely red, and even some spikes will only have a small portion of yellow coloring, while others on the same plant will show remarkable variegation. 35 cents each.

Maiden's Blush, has proven one of the most popular kinds. It is pronounced by experts pure soft pink, an indescribable tint of day-dawn loveliness, entirely different from all others. It is an immense bloomer and bears splendid trusses of exquisite lily-like flowers continuously all through the summer and fall until killed down by frost. 25 cents each.

Mrs. Noel Martin, very large flowers with large carmine petals, passing to rose carmine with touches of clear yellow. Splendid habit, with fine trusses, a novelty. 50 cents each.

Paul Burant, a beautiful crimson canna with dark foliage. Produces large flowers.

Florence Vaughan, flowers very large and broad, yellow-spotted bright scarlet; free bloomer and strong habit. This is one of the best varieties in cultivation.

Charles Henderson, a very fine red variety, which blooms all summer.

Pennsylvania, one of the best of the Italian hybrids, with flowers 6½ inch in diameter, produced with remarkable freedom in many branches and panicles of intense vermillion scarlet overlaid with a orange scarlet sheen. Rich, massive, deep green foliage, 6 to 7 feet. 20 cents each.

Pres. Viger, a splendid variety in dark scarlet with extraordinarily large florets, which are often borne in three distinct spikes on one flower stem. About 4 feet high. 50 cents each.

Wm. Bofinger, large, broad, massive foliage of bright green, and rich scarlet flowers overlaid with glowing orange scarlet, a color that can be seen as far as the eye will carry. One of the brightest and most attractive colors we have seen. The plant is of strong habit, growing about 5 feet high, very free flowering and decided acquisition. 25 cents each.

West Grove, rich green foliage, and is an exceedingly strong, vigorous grower. The flowers are large, very well shaped and their substance is something remarkable. The color is a rich coral pink, slightly dappled with a bright crimson and shaded with yellow in the throat. 25 cents each.

Gladiolus.

Bulbs extra large, 1½ to 2 inches in diameter, of the finest varieties that money can buy, 5 cents each; 50 cents per 12; $2.50 per 100.

The gladiolus blooms only once, and although its beauty only lasts a short time, it is beloved by everybody who knows it. The flowers are borne on spikes 2 to 3 feet long, and bloom in succession for about 8 to 14 days, the lower flowers blooming first. To have a continuance of bloom the bulbs ought to be planted at intervals every two weeks, from March first until the end of May. My bulbs are extra large, well matured and taken only from the finest varieties.

Die Gladiolus blüht nur einmal, doch ist die Blüthe eine wahre Pracht da jeder Stengel eine andere Farbe oder Schattirung hervorbringt. Um lange Zeit von diesen prächtigen Blumen zu haben, sollte man Knollen im März, April und Mai pflanzen. Meine Knollen sind groß und gesund und die feinste Mischung, die zu haben ist.

Try a hundred of my extra large and extra fine bulbs, and have the grandest flower you ever saw of all colors, Yellow, Crimson, Buff, Salmon, Lemon, Pink, Rose, White, Maroon, Cherry, Scarlet, and in fact all oddly marked sorts that one can think of.

Tuberoses. In tender beauty and delicious fragrance this lovely flower has no equal. It is easy to grow, and quick and sure to bloom. I have the three best varieties, Dwarf Excelsior Pearl, Orange Flowered and New Variegated leaved. 10 cents each, $1.00 per dozen, $7.50 per 100.

Tritoma Everblooming, the greatest bedding plant ever introduced, surpassing the finest cannas for attractiveness and brilliancy, equal to the gladiolus as a cut flower and blooms incessantly from June until December. Plants hardy in open ground. Strong roots, 15 cents each.

Flowering Plants.

Cactus Dahlia, another beautiful perennial of great magnificence, raising its brilliantly colored flowers on lofty stems. We have only the very latest European varieties, and a mixture of all the different colors. 5 cents per bulb, 50 cents per dozen.

Paeonies, magnificent hardy plants, almost rivaling the rose in brilliancy of color and perfection of bloom. They thrive in almost any soil or situation. 25 cents per bulb.

Hardy Garden Pinks, very hardy variety of pinks used for fringing flower beds. They are very sweet scented, and of various colors. 5 cents each, 50 cents per dozen.

CARNATIONS.

The Carnation excels all other flowers, the rose alone excepted. If planted in the open ground it will bloom all summer, and if taken out and brought indoors at the approach of cold weather, it will bloom in winter.

I have grown very strong plants in the open field, which were well hardened, and which have bloomed here.

Mixed Colors (Seedlings), grown from the very best Italian seeds. 5 cents each, 40 cents per dozen.

Carnations, in named varieties, crimson, red, white, pink and variegated of the most popular varieties. 15 cents each, $1.50 per dozen.

Luxome Violets, a new violet with flowers as large as those of the California Violets, but of much sweeter order. Have found this to be the only violet which stands the hot weather in summer well. 5 cents each, 40 cents per dozen, $3.00 per 100.

Giant Flowering Pansies, (Viola Tricolor Maxima). I have imported the finest mixed pansy seed that I could get in Europe, and have very strong plants to offer of the same, at 15 cents per dozen, $1.00 per 100.

Caladium Esculentum, (Elephant Ears), one of the most effective plants in cultivation for the flower border, or for planting out upon the lawn.

It will grow in any good garden soil and is of the easiest culture, but to obtain the best results it should be planted in rich compost and plentifully supplied with water. 15 cents each, 4 for 50 cents.

BANANA. (MUSA).

This is the most beautiful foliage plant that can be grown outside of the hot-house. Grand for bedding out in the summer, or for conservatory, or window decoration. Can be kept unwatered in a cellar over winter. 30 cents each, 3 for 75 cents.

Flower Seeds.

All the flower seeds that I offer are guranteed to be fresh and of the very highest standard quality. These seeds have been imported by myself from Italy (except those where otherwise stated) and I tested them as soon as they arrived here.

Balsams, improved rose, extra double, 10 cents per package.

Dianthus Chinensis, Chinese pinks, very best mixed, 5 cents per package.

Garden Pinks, single and double and all different colors mixed, 5 cents per package (home grown seed).

Dahlia Variabilis, double mixed, 10 cents per package.

Margaret Carnations, dwarf mixed, brilliant colors, 10 cents per package.

Japanese Morning Glory, 5 cents per package (home grown).

Coxcomb, best mixed, 5 cents per package (home grown).

Phlox Drummondii, best mixed, 5 cents per package.

Cypress Vine, a most beautiful climber, with delicate dark green, feathery foliage, and an abundance of bright, star-shaped, scarlet and white blossoms, 5 cents per package (home grown).

Verbenas, giant flowered, 5 cents per package.

Winter Stocks, mixture of all colors, 10 cents per package.

Zinnias, all colors mixed, 5 cents per package (home grown).

VEGETABLE SEEDS.

Tomato, Leicester's Prolific. I have found this to be the best bearer of all the large-fruited tomatoes. The quality of the fruit is the very best. Color is very attractive. 10 cents per package.

Cucumber Prince, a cucumber which is nearly all flesh, and of excellent quality; never gets bitter. Smooth and round, and easy to peel. 10 cents per package.

Lady Peas, a very productive pea which can be planted as late as July here. Peas white, very small, but the best eating pea known. 10 cents per pound, $3.00 per bushel.

Cow Peas, for forage or as restorer of nitrogen to poor soils. 10 cents per pound, $1.50 per bushel.

WATER MELON SEEDS.

We have saved the seeds of the finest specimen water melon, all mixed seeds, which are the best melons for planting here. We offer the mixture at 10 cents per ounce, $1.50 per pound.

Holbert Honey, is the sweetest and finest of all melons. In quality it is simply delicious, sugary, and of a frinty flavor, peculiar to itself. Entirely devoid of all fibrous substances, the sweet flesh melting away in the mouth like honey. The hardy vines are wonderfully prolific. It is very early and the best melon I have ever tested. 10 cents per package, 25 cents per ounce.

SEED CORN.

I. & G. N. Corn. At the Fair in San Antonio in October, 1902 I found a few ears of the soft fine white corn at the I. & G. N. exhibit and the company presented it to me for trial. It is a pure white soft corn, grows 7 to 9 feet high and bears two extra large ears, with long, soft, white grains which make an excellent white meal, seed at $2.00 per bushel.

Mexican June Corn, this corn will bring a good crop if planted at any time from April to middle of June. It stands our hot, dry summer well, and the seed I offer is grown by me and adapted to our climate, and will bring the best results. $1.50 per bushel.

SWEET POTATOES.

Southern Queen, early and very productive, grows large, a yellowish white color, cooks very dry, grows short and smooth. One peculiarity about this variety is its short, thick vines, usually 2 to 3 feet in length.

Purple Yam, an old standard sort, also known as red Spanish or nigger choker, with dark purplish-red vines of vigorous habit; potatoes dark red outside, inner skin deep crimson, with white, solid, sweet flesh, keeps well and is a great yielder.

Price, per bushel for seed $1.00.

Can supply any demand for vines after June the 1st, at the following price. Purple Yams, 40 cents per 100, $3.50 per 1000; Southern Queen, 35 cents per 100; $3.00 per 1000.

Pruning Shears, Wiss, hand-made. These are the best Pruning Shears made, No. 109, 9 inches long, $2.25 each; No. 110, 10 inches long, $2.50 each.

FOR THOSE WHO IRRIGATE.

I have a special lot of peach and plum trees which are all of bearing age, and which are worth just so much more to the planter than his land is worth to him in two years. It saves just two years of growing the trees in an orchard by getting these large trees. They have a low stem, a well balanced top, and a perfect system of roots. These are not trees which have been left over from previous years, but they are trees which I have grown especially for those of my customers who irrigate. The young twigs of last years growth are full of fruit buds, and should be cut back to about one-third their size upon receipt of trees, which leaves several fruit buds on each twig, and at the same time there will be plenty of new wood formed for next year's fruit crop.

The cost of these trees is but very little more than the cost of a small tree, and besides saving you two years of growing in your orchard, it saves the trouble of forming a well balanced top. For prices on small lots see this catalogue, and for prices on big lots of these trees kindly write to us.

PROPER DISTANCES OF PLANTING.

Peach, Apricots, Nectarines	12 to 16 feet each way
Plums, Cherries	10 to 15 feet each way
Pears	18 to 20 feet each way
Persimmons	10 to 12 feet each way
Apples	16 to 20 feet each way
Grapes	6 to 8 feet each way

Dewberries and Blackberries, rows 4 to 6 feet apart, 2 feet in row.

NUMBER OF TREES OR PLANTS TO THE ACRE.

Distance apart	No. of Trees
3x3 feet	4,840
6x6 feet	1,210
8x8 feet	680
10x10 feet	435
12x12 feet	302
15x15 feet	193
16x16 feet	170
18x18 feet	134
20x20 feet	108
25x25 feet	69

Below I describe a few insecticides for destroying insects, rots, San Jose Scale and all contagious diseases. I have been using these insecticides for many years and can cheerfully recommend them to all of my customers, who have had trouble in their orchards and farms by insects and plant diseases.

Birds are getting less and less every year and insects more and it has become necessary to destroy them by spraying.

The price for insecticides is f. o. b. New Braunfels, Texas, and is just what it cost us.

PRICES ON BOWKERS' GERMO-INSECTICIDES.

BOXAL, a combined insecticide and fungicide for use on potatoes, kills bugs and beetles, and prevents blight and rot; takes the place of Paris green and Bordeaux mixture, and is superior to both. Sticks to the vines throughout the season. 5 pound can 60 cents.

PYROX, a combined insecticide and fungicide for use on fruit trees, shrubs and vines. Kills leaf and fruit eating insects and prevents scab, rot, mildew, etc. Superior to Bordeaux and Paris green, safer and more effective. Sticks and "works all the time." 5 pound can 90 cents.

BODO, a valuable remedy for rot, rust, blight and fungous diseases in general; of great strength and much superior to home-made Bordeaux mixture. Ready for use when needed. 5 pound can 60 cents.

DISPARENE, the most powerful remedy for all leaf eating insects; will not injure foliage, and adheres throughout the season. 2 pound can 60 cents.

TREE SOAP, a sure remedy for the San Jose Scale and all other scales or lice on plants or trees. Contains caustic potash. 5 pound can 60 cents.

INSECT EMULSION, a clean and cheap remedy for lice, house plants or animals. 1 quart can 60 cents.

BODLIME, prevents moths, caterpillars and other insects from ascending trees. A substitute for printer's ink. 5 pound can 90 cents.

DISINFECTANT, a powerful antiseptic and disinfectant. Kills germs, prevents disease, heals cuts and sores on man or beast.

If large quantities are desired will furnish prices on application.

Testimonials.

Receiving bushels of nice letters from our customers, we have picked out a few, which have all been recently written, and which need no further explanation, because they explain themselves. Look them over and you will find that they are all from prominent farmers and business men and they show how well pleased our customers are with our trees, plants and good packing.

MARATHON, TEXAS, March 28, 1903.

Mr. Otto Locke, New Braunfels, Texas:
Dear Sir and Friend.—Find bill of trees to be shipped on December the 20th. My trees I got from you are all doing well, especially the Japan plums.
Your friend,
JOHN STILLWELL.

NOTRE DAME, INDIANA, April 22, 1903.

Mr. Otto Locke, New Braunfels, Texas:
Dear Sir.—I take the liberty to write to you, to let you know how my roses (that you had the kindness of sending in February) are getting along. I wish you could see them. They have surpassed everything that I or anyone else, at least in Notre Dame, has ever seen. Especially the Kaiserin Aug. Vict. which has grown 25 inches since February and has three magnificent, large, sweet scented flowers and it is the admiration of all.
I shall have a notice of your roses in our college paper and will send you a copy. I remain dear sir, yours truly,
BROTHER FREDERICK.

SAN ANTONIO, TEXAS, March 25, 1903.

Mr. Otto Locke, New Braunfels, Texas:
Dear Sir.—The trees arrived yesterday in a good condition, they have all been planted and are looking nicely. Many thanks for the extra trees.
Yours sincerely,
ARTHUR DIETRICH.

SEGUIN, TEXAS, March 4, 1903.

Mr. Otto Locke, New Braunfels, Texas:
Dear Sir.—It is with pleasure that I acknowledge receipt of trees ordered and also the fair treatment accorded me. Not only was the fulfillment of order more than expected but the excellent condition of trees upon arrival left nothing to be desired and I can cheerfully recommend you to any one contemplating the purchase of anything in your line.
Very respectfully,
DR. F. B. TEGNER.

PEARSALL, TEXAS, April 9, 1903.

Mr. Otto Locke, New Braunfels, Texas:
Dear Sir.—Enclosed find check to cover your bill of March 5, which please place to my credit.
Please send me one of your catalogues, the roses, privets, etc., that I bought of you are doing well.
Yours very truly,
JOHN M. KEMPER.

BIG SPRINGS, TEXAS, November 30, 1902.

Mr Otto Locke, New Braunfels, Texas:
Dear Sir.—Enclosed please find money order for $1.95. I received the last lot of trees in good condition, they are all fine looking trees and that is the reason I am not satisfied yet, and am sending for a few more.
If you are going to put in anything extra then put in a few plants for my wife.
Yours truly,
R. SCHWARZENBACH.

SAN ANTONIO, TEXAS, December 22, 1902.
Mr. Otto Locke, New Braunfels, Texas:
Dear Sir:—Trees and plants received in extra good condition and am well pleased with them and have planted everything. Will give you an order for roses in a few days.

Yours truly,
J. M. VANCE.

BALLINGER, TEXAS, December 12, 1902.
Mr. Otto Locke, New Braunfels, Texas:
Dear Sir: I have received the trees and shrubs, and have them all nicely set out. I am sure they will all grow. I was well pleased with the order and will take pleasure in recommending your nursery to any one that I think will want anything in your line, with many thanks for your kindness.

Respectfully,
H. A. CADY,
P. M., Ballinger, Texas.

SAN MARCOS, TEXAS.
Mr. Otto Locke, New Braunfels, Texas:
Dear Sir: Please sign enclosed voucher, and return. I enclose franked envelope. Thanks for the extra roses, all plants were fine and in good condition.

Very truly,
JOHN L. LEARY.

DALLAS, TEXAS, February 1, 1903.
Mr. Otto Locke, New Braunfels, Texas:
Kind Sir: Accept my thanks for your prompt attention in filling my order. All trees arrived in first-class condition and we will gladly give you our future trade. Praise in this vicinity.

Yours truly,
MAX GRONAU.

P. S. Your catalogue has already changed hands, was borrowed third day after arrival. Max Gronau.

AUSTIN, TEXAS, February 7, 1903.
Mr. Otto Locke, New Braunfels, Texas:
Dear Sir: Yours of the 26th, received and will say in reply that everything is O. K. I feel very proud of my trees, and believe I will have good luck with same, as the season is very favorable for tree planting this year.
I will begin setting out at once and hope to have them all transplanted before it rains again. Should you ever come to Austin in the near future please call on me and I will show you the nicest 20 acres of land in the state.
Wishing you and your family good health and a prosperous year, and thanking you very much for the kindness and indulgence you have shown me, and also for the extra fine trees, I am with many good wishes for your future success.

Yours respectfully,
AUG. WEILBACHER, JR.

P. S. Mr. Weilbacher planted over 1000 of our bearing age trees. Otto Locke.

SAN ANTONIO, TEXAS, January 10, 1903.
Mr. Otto Locke, New Braunfels, Texas:
Dear Sir: Enclosed you will find my check for $5.90 to cover amount due for trees. I am more than pleased with the condition of the trees upon their arrival, in the manner of packing and fine appearance and quality of the trees.

Yours very truly,
ALBERT FRIEDERICH.

LEON SPRINGS, TEXAS.
Mr. Otto Locke, New Braunfels, Texas:
Dear Sir: The fruit trees I ordered from you arrived yesterday in good shape. Have planted them already. Many thanks for your prompt attention. Trees turned out to satisfaction. I shall with pleasure recommend your nursery to everyone. With kind regards,

Yours truly,
M. AUE.

LOCKHART, TEXAS, January 12, 1903.

Mr. Otto Locke, New Braunfels, Texas:

Dear Sir: Received the trees. I am well pleased with them. Many thanks.

Yours respectfully,

JOS. COLLING.

CASTROVILLE, TEXAS, March 3, 1903.

Mr. Otto Locke, New Braunfels, Texas:

Dear Sir: Plants received in good order. Many thanks for the extra ones. Was well pleased with everything.

Respectfully,

T. F. FITZ-SIMON, M. D.

GRASSYVILLE, TEXAS, January 20, 1903.

Mr. Otto Locke, New Braunfels, Texas:

Dear Sir:—I wish to acknowledge receipt of flowers, etc., all in good order. I feel that I am obliged to you on account of your generous dealing with me. For the present accept my thanks. I shall not fail to recommend your nursery whenever I have a chance to do so.

Yours truly,

(REV.) E. A. KOKEN.

LAREDO, TEXAS.

Mr. Otto Locke, New Braunfels, Texas:

Dear Sir: We received the plants you sent and are very much pleased with them. Thanking you for kindness, I remain,

Yours truly,

(Mrs.) A. McDONALD.

SAN ANTONIO, TEXAS, February 2, 1903.

Mr. Otto Locke, New Braunfels, Texas:

Dear Sir: Your package received, and I wish to thank you for the trees. I am well pleased with them. Have given the catalogue to several parties and will recommend you whenever I can.

Yours respectfully,

(Mrs.) J. SCHWEPPE.

UVALDE, TEXAS.

Mr. Otto Locke, New Braunfels, Texas:

Dear Sir:—Enclosed find stamps for which please send me tomato seed (Licester's Prolific). I used tht seed last year and the tomato is simply grand. Send at once and oblige,

Yours truly,

(Mrs.) C. W. WATT.

SAN ANTONIO, TEXAS, March 9, 1903.

Mr. Otto Locke, New Braunfels, Texas:

Dear Sir: Your trees and shrubs arrived in due time. They were very satisfactory and many, many thanks for the generous package for the "House of the Good Shepard." This is a late date to acknowledge the favors, but, better late then never. One of my neighbors has patronized you, through my order being O. K., and I will do some advertising for your nursery later. It is too late for the spring planting but will look out for the fall of 1904, then you will get good sales here

Respectfully,

(Miss) MARY A. CAMPBELL.

NOPAL, TEXAS.

Mr. Otto Locke, New Braunfels, Texas:

Dear Sir:—I wish to thank you for the trees and vines which I received alright and in due time. They were much better than I had expected. I am well pleased with them and think they are all growing. Will order from you in the future.

Respectfully,

SAM SMALLY.

EL PASO, TEXAS.

Mr. Otto Locke, New Braunfes, Texas:

Dear Sir:—The trees came in perfect condition and are just what I wanted. I now enclose $10.00 for another dozen prepaid, from 4 to 5 feet of a bright green variety. Thanking you for last shipment.

Yours respectfully,

(Mrs.) BRITTON DAVIS

SAN ANTONIO, TEXAS, January 6, 1903.

Mr. Otto Locke, New Braunfels, Texas:

Dear Sir: Many thanks for the beautiful trees. We are delighted with them and are already enjoying the anticipation of much fruit this year and so many varieties.

We thank you also for the extra trees you sent, and the freight charges were only 55 cents on them.

All are planted and as we expect all to grow and do well will send for additional trees every year. Wishing you happiness and success during the new year, I am,
Yours respectfully,
(Mrs.) COL. W. T. MECHLING.

COPP'S FARM AND GARDEN RANCH,
COTULLA, TEXAS.

Mr. Otto Locke, New Braunfels, Texas:

Dear Sir: The rose bushes received. They were in fine condition. I shall recommend your nursery to all my friends. Yours truly,
(Mrs.) GEO. COPP.

DUNLAY, TEXAS, February 2, 1903.

Mr. Otto Locke, New Braunfels, Texas:

Dear Sir: The bill of fruit trees bought of you were received on the 22nd, and will say, they opened to my entire satisfaction. I was very much pleased with them. You send out finer trees than any nursery I have ever bought from. In fact so many have proven to be such frauds. The bill I bought of you I had priced to me by another nurseryman much below what you had priced them at, but I was afraid to trust my order with them, so I forwarded my order to the Comal Springs Nursery knowing you to be honest in your line of business.

Yes, I will recommend your nursery to my friends with the greatest pleasure. I will assure you that as long as you send out as fine trees as I have seen from your nursery, your trade will grow to be immensely large in a very short while. Wishing you success, I am. Yours truly,
L. J. SCHMIDT.

Quality and not quantity is our "motto."—Otto Locke.

TORREON, COAH, MEXICO, March 26, 1903.

Mr. Otto Locke, New Braunfels, Texas:

Dear Sir: Herewith please find draft No. 2540 in your favor for amount due you for the trees, I received them in good condition. Accept thanks.
Yours truly,
E. JACKSON

MAXWELL, TEXAS, December 12, 1902.

Mr. Otto Locke, New Braunfels, Texas:

Dear Sir: Please find enclosed money order to cover bill. I am more than pleased with the trees and roses. Thanks. H. HARTMANN.

CASTROVILLE, TEXAS. January 17, 903.

Mr. Otto Locke, New Braunfels, Texas:

Dear Sir: The Nursery stock arrived all O. K. Please accept my thanks for the promptness with which you attended to my order. I enclose receipt to cover your advertising for this season and thank you for your patronage. I shall take pleasure in recommending your nursery to my friends.
Yours truly,
FLETCHER DAVIS.
Prop. The Anvil.

KENEDY, TEXAS, January 8, 1903.

Mr. Otto Locke, New Braunfels, Texas:

Dear Sir: The plants received Tuesday, am very well pleased with them. I shall recommend your nursery to my friends.
Yours respectfully,
(Miss) DELLA BUTLER.

BRACKETTVILLE, TEXAS, February 27, 1903.

Mr. Otto Locke, New Braunfels, Texas:
  Dear Sir: The last shipment received all O. K. The ladies and myself were very well pleased with the roses.
  Have given your book to quite a number of ladies and they will all favor you with their orders.

Yours respectfully,
MRS. WM. SHARP.

———

MARATHON, TEXAS, Februar 3, 1903.

Mr. Otto Locke, New Braunfels, Texas:
  Dear Sir: I today mail you another order for rose bushes and fruit trees. I received the foregoing shipment in a splendid condition, and all who saw them were perfectly carried away with them. I loaned my catalogue to a neighbor who wants to plant 50 or more trees from you. Thanking you for promptness.

Yours respectfully
MRS. LUCY CRAWFORD.

———

SAN ANTONIO, TEXAS, May 27, 1903.

Mr. Otto Locke, New Braunfels, Texas:
  Dear Sir: Enclosed find my check in payment of bill, everything came alright and all plants are growing nicely. Thanking you for same.

Yours very truly,
L. B. CLEGG.

———

LAREDO, TEXAS, February 28, 1903.

Mr. Otto Locke, New Braunfels, Texas:
  Dear Sir: Mrs. Worsham received the roses and both ladies were much pleased with them. Herewith money order for enclosed lot of fruit trees. I am instructed to thank you for the extra roses sent with former order and that she will recommend your nursery at every opportunity.

I am hurridly, yours, etc.,
THOMAS WORSHAM, JR.

———

SAN ANTONIO, TEXAS, January 29, 1903.

Mr. Otto Locke, New Braunfels, Texas:
  Dear Sir: Enclosed please find check for $17.30 in payment of bill which please receipt and return.
  I am very well pleased with the trees you sent me and will gladly put in a good word for you whenever I can.

Yours truly,
J. A. DUERLER.

———

NOTRE DAME, INDIANA, March 29, 1903.

Mr. Otto Locke, New Braunfels, Texas:
  My Dear Friend: The roses came in splendid condition, and I have been getting roses from other houses before, but never in such a good condition as yours. Please send me the roses given below.
  Brother Frederick thinks there are no roses like you have. He sends his regards. With best wishes, your sincere friend,
SISTER M. ALOYSIUS.

———

ROSANKY, TEXAS, June 17, 1903.

Mr. Otto Locke, New Braunfels, Texas:
  Dear Sir: The trees I got from you are the best I ever set out and whenever I want any more I will order them from you only. I set them out in February and every one is growing nicely, some of them have large peaches on them.
  All my neighbors who see them, say the trees are fine.

Yours very truly,
A. E. MEUTH.

Zeugnisse.

Lacoste, Texas, den 13. Juni 1903.

Werther Herr!

Hiermit muß ich Ihnen mittheilen, daß alle Bäume, welche ich von Ihnen bezogen habe, prächtig gedeihen. Besonders die Birnbäume vom letzten Winter, welche ich auf neues Land gepflanzt habe, wachsen ausgezeichnet.

Mit Gruß

Wm. Geiger.

Schulenburg, Texas, den 10. Juni 1903.

Werther Herr Locke!

Die Bäume von Ihnen wachsen alle sehr gut und sind alle gut angegangen. Auch waren wir mit der Sendung sehr zufrieden.

Achtungsvoll
Frau Adelheid Kiesewetter.

Yorttown, Texas, den 12. Juni 1903.

Geehrter Herr Locke!

Ich will Ihnen mittheilen, wie die Bäume, welche ich von Ihnen erhielt, gedeihen. Ich bin vollkommen zufrieden damit. Es ist eine Pracht, sie anzu= sehen. Pflaumen und Pfirsiche wachsen am vortrefflichsten und ich bekomme schon einige Proben von Bäumen, welche ich vergangenen Winter gepflanzt habe. Alle Bäume, die ich in 1901 pflanzte, stehen ausgezeichnet. Auch die Zier=Bäume auf dem Friedhofe wachsen prachtvoll, dieses beweist, daß man Ihre Bäume nur empfehlen kann, denn erstens sind sie viel billiger und zwei= tens wachsen sie viel besser, als solche, die vom Norden kommen und $1 das Stück kosten. Ich habe Ihren werthvollen Katalog schon viele meiner Freunde gegeben und weiß, daß einige bestellt haben und sie sind alle sehr zufrieden mit dem, was sie erhielten. Mit herzlichsten Gruß zeichnet, hochachtungsvoll,

Ernst Felch.

Clifton, Texas, den 14. Juni 1903.

Herrn Otto Locke, Neu=Braunfels, Texas.

Werther Freund!

Alle Bäume, welche ich dieses Frühjahr oder Winter von Ihnen bekom= men habe sind gut gewachsen, trotzdem sie am ersten Mai abgefroren waren, so kann man jetzt nichts mehr von Frost sehen und die Krone ist um so breiter ge= worden. Die Bäume empfehlen sich von selbst, denn Jeder, der mich besucht, frägt, wo hast Du die Bäume her? Bäume kaufen ist eine Vertrauenssache und ich für meinen Theil bin gerade auf dem Punkt angelangt, daß ich mir die Mühe nicht mehr gebe, einen Baum zu pflanzen von einem Agenten, den ich nicht kenne. Grüßt freundschaftlichst Ihr

August Arlitt.

Dallas, Texas, den 24. Januar 1903.

Werther Herr Locke!

Die Bäume und Rosen haben wir erhalten und sind gut zufrieden damit. Besten Dank für Ihre schöne Zugabe. Werden Ihre Baumschule aufs Beste empfehlen.

Achtungsvoll

Lucy Traves.

St. Bernard College, St. Bernard, Alabama

Herrn Otto Locke, Neu-Braunfels, Texas.

Geehrter Herr!

Vor einigen Jahren hat ein junger Mann von hier Bäume von Ihnen gekauft, welche in unserer Gegend sehr gut gedeihen. Wir sind sehr zufrieden damit und da ich auch welche von Ihnen beziehen möchte, so wäre es mir erwünscht, wenn Sie mir einen Ihrer Kataloge zusenden würden, denn ich denke das Ihre Bäume am besten für unsere Lage geeignet sind. . Achtungsvoll

Fr. Aemilian.

Yorktown, Texas, den 2. Januar 1903.

Werther Herr Locke!

Die Rosen, Birnbäume 2c. vorgestern erhalten. Es sind alle starke, gesund ansehende Pflanzen. Besten Dank für die Zugabe.

Achtungsvoll

Robert Westphal, M. D.

Bastrop, Texas, den 3. Januar 1903.

Werther Herr Locke!

Ihre Bäume = Sendung erhalten und bin sehr zufrieden damit ; meinen besten Dank dafür. Ich habe es seit einem Jahre nicht daran fehlen lassen, Ihre Baumschule zu empfehlen, aber entweder sind die Leute zu unwissend oder zu bequem und lassen sich immer wieder durch Agenten anführen und bezahlen von 50 Cents bis $1 für California Seedlings.

Achtungsvoll

J. Keil.

Texarkana, Texas, den 15. Dezember 1902.

Werther Herr Locke!

Habe die Bäume erhalten und bin sehr gut damit zufrieden. Auch danke ich Ihnen verbindlichst für die Extra=Bäume, die Sie zugelegt haben.

Achtungsvoll

Joe Baumgartner.

Grassyville, Texas, den 17. Januar 1903.

Herrn Otto Locke, Neu-Braunfels, Texas.

Werther Herr!

Die mir zugesandten Bäume 2c. kamen wohlverpackt in gutem Zustand an. Ihre außerordentliche Liberalität bestimmt mich, Ihnen meinen verbindlichsten Dank auszudrücken. Ich erwartete in der Expreß = Office ein kleines Bündel für mich zu finden und war ganz verdutzt, als ich so viel wie 65 Cents für Expreß-Kosten bezahlen sollte; als ich aber den großen Bündel prächtiger Bäume sah, war ich ganz zufrieden. Beim Auspacken gab es noch eine Ueberraschung. Ihre Gratis-Zusendung deckt recht gut die Expreß = Kosten. Ihre Baumschule verdient alle Anpreisung.

Achtungsvoll

Rev. C. A. Konten.

Schulenburg, Texas, den 27. Januar 1903.

Werther Herr Locke!

Die Bäume erhalten. Besten Dank. Sind alle sehr gut angekommen. Habe Ihre Baumschule bestens empfohlen. So werden Sie wohl dieser Tage einige Aufträge von hier erhalten.

Achtungsvoll

Adelheid Kiesewetter.

Marion, Texas, den 10. November 1902.

Werther Herr Locke!

Beiliegend sende ich Ihnen eine Liste von Bäumen, welche ich pflanzen möchte; machen Sie mir gefälligst Preise darauf und ich werde gleich nach Empfang Ihrer Antwort den Betrag dafür einschicken. Die letztjährigen Bäume sind alle wunderschön.

Mit Gruß

Heinrich J. Behrens.

Engle, Texas, den 24. Januar 1903.

Herrn Otto Locke, Neu-Braunfels, Texas.

Geehrter Herr!

Ich habe die Bäume erhalten und muß gestehen, daß ich sehr zufrieden damit bin, denn es sind die besten, die ich je erhalten habe.

Achtungsvoll

Christ. Brüggmann.

Lytle, Texas, den 20. Februar 1903.

Werther Herr Locke!

Ich habe die Bäumchen in sehr gutem Zustande erhalten und ich bedanke mich für die Zugabe. Habe mich sehr darüber gefreut. Werde nächstes Jahr mehr bestellen.

Achtungsvoll

E. Ziegenbalg.

P. S.—Ich werde Ihre Baumschule meinen Nachbaren empfehlen.

Flatonia, Texas, den 12. November 1902.

Werther Herr Locke!

Vor acht Jahren kaufte ich eine Anzahl Fruchtbäume von Ihnen, mit denen ich sehr zufrieden war. Beiliegend finden Sie wieder eine kleine Bestellung; die Auswahl überlasse ich Ihnen.

Achtungsvoll

A. Bittner.

Marwell, Texas, den 11. Februar 1903.

Herrn Otto Locke, Neu-Braunfels, Texas.

Werther Herr!

Die von Ihnen bestellten Rosenstöcke nebst Veilchen ꝛc. in guter Verpackung erhalten. Die Rosen sind Pracht-Exemplare für das Geld; auch die anderen Blumenstöcke sind groß und schön. Ich war wirklich überrascht, hatte mir so große und prachtvolle Stöcke nicht vorgestellt. Werde Ihre Baumschule empfehlen, wo ich nur kann. Besten Dank.

Achtungsvoll

A. C. Münter.

Grassvville, März 1903.

Herrn Otto Locke, Neu-Braunfels, Texas.

Werther Herr!

Ich habe Ihre letzte Sendung in gutem Zustand erhalten. Alles ist mehr wie befriedigend. Besten Dank für die gratis Zugesandten. Bitte senden Sie mir noch einen Katalog, da ich meinen an einen Nachbar verborgt und Sie bestens empfohlen habe.

Achtungsvoll

C. A. Konten.

Taylor, Texas, den 19. Dezember 1902.

Herrn Otto Locke!

Habe die Bäume erhalten und bin sehr gut damit zufrieden. Solche Bäume von solch guter Qualität habe ich noch nie erhalten von anderen Baumschulen. Ich freute mich sehr darüber, habe alle gleich gepflanzt. Werde Ihre Baumschule bestens empfehlen. Nehmen Sie meinen verbindlichsten Dank für gute Bedienung.   Mit Gruß Achtungsvoll

Henry Fritz.

Engle, Texas, den 7. Dezember 1902.

Herrn Otto Locke, Neu-Braunfels, Texas.

Werther Herr!

Habe die Bäume erhalten und bin gut damit zufried n. Werde Ihnen dieser Tage einen Auftrag für meinen Nachbar senden.   Achtungsvoll

Jos. Kierlich.

Birch, Texas, den 23. Dezember 1902.

Werther Herr Locke!

Ich habe die Bäume in bester Ordnung erhalten und sage Ihnen hiermit meinen besten Dank. Ich werde Ihre Baumschule an alle meine Freunde empfehlen.   Achtungsvoll

C. A. Heinte.

Loreno, Texas, den 24. Dezember 1902.

Herrn Otto Locke, Neu-Braunfels, Texas.

Geehrter Herr!

Ich habe die Bäume, die ich von Ihnen bestellt hatte, richtig erhalten und bin sehr zufrieden damit. Vielen Dank für die Extras. Ich werde Ihre Baumschule Jedermann empfehlen.   Hochachtungsvoll

A. T. Guderian.

Dunlay, Texas, den 10. Januar 1903.

Werther Herr!

Habe die Bäume in bestem Zustande erhalten; hatte nicht erwartet so starke Bäume zu erhalten. Besten Dank dafür. Werde nächsten Winter für Ihre Baumschule Reklame machen.   Mit Gruß

Jakob Breiten.

P. S. Die Bäume, die wir vor vier Jahren von Ihnen erhielten, gedeihen vortrefflich und haben alle gut getragen.   J. B.

Austin, Texas, den 31. Januar 1903.

Herrn Otto Locke, Neu-Braunfels, Texas.

Werther Herr!

Die Bäume habe ich richtig erhalten. Ich bin sehr zufrieden damit. Es sind alles prachtvolle Bäume. Werde Ihre Bäume empfehlen, wo ich nur kann. Sie sind mir vor zwei Jahren von Herrn Schütze empfohlen worden und so werde ich Sie weiter empfehlen, welches ich mit gutem Gewissen thun kann. Sie werden auch jetzt eine Bestellung durch mich erhalten. Wenn Sie nach Austin kommen und Ihre Zeit es erlaubt, bitte mich zu besuchen. Auch möchte ich noch um einen Katalog bitten, da ich meinen in Ihrem Interesse weggegeben habe. Hiermit nehmen Sie meinen besten Dank auch für die Extra-Bäume. Es zeichnet mit aller Hochachtung Ihr ergebenster

C. Düsterhöft.

Reedville, Texas, den 25. Februar 1903.

Herrn Otto Locke, Neu-Braunfels, Texas.

Werther Herr!

Die Bäume nebst Rechnung in bester Ordnung erhalten, wofür Sie Money Order finden. Besten Dank.

Achtungsvoll

Willie Kowald.

Carmine, Texas, den 17. Oktober 1902.

Herrn Otto Locke!

Beiliegend eine kleine Bestellung für Sämereien. Aller Samen und Pflanzen, die wir leptes Jahr erhielten, sind gut und geben volle Zufriedenheit.

Achtungsvoll

Frl. Ella Mayer.

Schulenburg, Texas, den 16. November 1902.

Werther Herr!

Ich hatte in 1900 Bäume von Ihnen bezogen, falls Sie sich noch erinnern und wollte für weitere Bestellung warten bis die Bäume getragen. Sie brachten mir dieses Jahr die erste Frucht; sie war wunderschön und deshalb bestelle ich mehr Bäume. Ich weiß jept, wo man die besten Bäume bekommen kann.

Achtungsvoll

Fred. Diettrich.

Shiner, Texas, den 22. November 1902.

Herrn Otto Locke, Neu-Braunfels, Texas.

Werther Herr!

Ihren Brief sowie Bäume erhalten und bin sehr zufrieden damit; meinen besten Dank und werde Ihre Baumschule stets empfehlen, und sollte ich später wieder etwas gebrauchen, dann werde ich nur bei Ihnen bestellen.

Mit Gruß, Achtungsvoll

Louis Ehlers.

Rutledge, Texas, den 12. Dezember 1902.

Herrn Otto Locke!

Hiermit die Mittheilung, daß die Sendung Fruchtbäume in bester Verfassung angekommen ist. Die Verpackung war ausgezeichnet, wie auch die Bäume. Auch meinen verbindlichsten Dank für das schöne Geschenk, welches gratis beigelegt war.

Mit freundlichem Gruß

Chas. Petri.

Marvell, Arkansas, den 14. Dezember 1902.

Werther Herr!

Ich habe die Bäume erhalten und bin mehr wie zufrieden damit. Ich habe wohl $5.65 Fracht bezahlen müssen, aber dennoch sind die Bäume viel billiger, als die, welche meine Nachbaren von Reisenden erhalten. Ich will nach Neujahr noch Reben und Brombeeren anpflanzen.

Mit Gruß

Al. Schaffhonser.

Weesatche, Texas, den 24. Dezember 1902.

Werther Herr Locke!

Ihr Schreiben sowie Bäume in gutem Zustande erhalten und bin sehr zufrieden damit und danke bestens für gute Behandlung.

Mit Gruß

Otto Gotschalt.

An meine deutschen Kunden.

Ich möchte besonders meinen Dank aussprechen für das große Vertrauen, welches Sie mir im letztvergangenen Geschäftsjahre entgegengebracht haben, ganz besonders Ihnen habe ich meinen Erfolg zu verdanken, so daß ich gezwungen bin wieder meine Baumschule zu vergrößern und größere Verbesserungen anzulegen und werde ich im Stande sein, in kommender Saison meine Kunden wieder mit dem Allerbesten zu versehen, sowie darauf bestrebt sein mir immer mehr Freunde und Gönner zu erwerben. Mein Prinzip ist, nicht nur für mich und meine Tasche zu arbeiten, sondern zum Wohle meiner Kunden und ist mir ein zufriedener Kunde viel lieber, als eine Tasche voll Dollar. Wie früher werde ich auch in Zukunft darauf sehen, daß ein Jeder mehr erhält, als er erwartet und das, was er erhält auch zu seinem Vortheil und Freude sein wird.

Sollten nun Fehler bei Füllung der Bestellung vorkommen oder Bäume nicht so sein, wie sie bestellt waren, so muß die Beschwerde innerhalb 5 Tagen nach Empfang der Bäume eingesandt werden und ich werde dann Alles zur vollen Zufriedenheit meiner Kunden recht machen. Ich halte mich aber nicht verantwortlich, wenn Bäume durch die Nachlässigkeit der Expreß Company Schaden leiden oder durch Insekten, Dürre ꝛc. zu Grunde gehen.

Die beste, sicherste und schnellste Art, Baumschul-Artikel zu versenden, ist immer per Express und nur bei sehr großen Aufträgen sollte bei Fracht bestellt werden.

Alle Bäume, die durch mich versandt werden, sind so verpackt, daß sie ohne Schaden zu leiden, eine Reise von drei Wochen aushalten können. Solche Wunderbäume wie „California Seedlings," die das ganze Jahr reife Früchte tragen oder Bäume, die auf Mesquite veredelt sind und ewig lebend oder Rosen, welche blaue oder grüne Blüthen hervorbringen, Weinstöcke und Stachelbeeren, welche Beeren so groß wie Hühner = Eier tragen und die $1 bis $5 das Stück kosten, führe ich nicht. Diese sehr werthvollen Neuheiten überlasse ich gerne dem zu gewandten zungengewubten Baum-Agenten, welcher ja auch leben will und leidernoch immer genug findet von Denen, die nie alle werden.

Dieses Jahr habe ich einen Vorrath von allen größen Bäumen von 12 Zoll an bis zu einem starken dreijährigen Baume, der gleich nach dem Verpflanzen Früchte tragen wird und kann ich diese Bäume, besonders für Diejenigen empfehlen, welche bewässern können.

Denjenigen meiner lieben Kunden, welche gute Ackerbau = Schriften wünschen empfehle ich „Feld und Flur", Dallas, Texas, 50 Cents per Jahr oder Denjenigen, welche lieber Englisch lesen „Claridge's Texas Stock Farmer", Lock Box L, San Antonio, Texas, Preis $1 per Jahr. Ferner Beide Blätter zusammen werde ich für $1 auf ein Jahr senden. Ferner empfehle ich folgende gute Wochenblätter

Texas Vorwärts, Austin, Texas, ...$2.00
Freie Presse für Texas, San Antonio, ... 2.50
Katholische Rundschau, San Antonio, ... 2.00
Bellville Wochenblatt, Bellville, Texas, ... 2.00

Hoffend, daß dieser Katalog alle meine Gönner gesund und munter erreicht, zeichnet, hochachtungsvoll

Otto Locke.

www.ingramcontent.com/pod-product-compliance
Lightning Source LLC
Chambersburg PA
CBHW021631270326
41931CB00008B/970